Wayne Visser
Clem Sunter

Beyond
Reasonable
Greed:
Why
Sustainable
Business
is a Much
Better Idea!

HUMAN & ROUSSEAU

TAFELBERG

Published jointly by Human & Rousseau
and Tafelberg Publishers,
both 28 Wale Street, Cape Town

Designed by Jürgen Fomm
and typeset in 11.5 on 14 pt Palatino
Printed and bound by Paarl Print,
Oosterland Street, Paarl, South Africa
First edition, first impression July 2002

ISBN 0 7981 4269 3

THIS BOOK IS DEDICATED TO

*Our families, for nurturing the elephant
    instinct in us;*
*The others in the herd who have inspired us;
    and*
*Those who professionally assisted us
    in trumpeting this message.*

There is a lone hill somewhere,
Without an elephant on it.
People yearned for an
elephant on that hill,
In time their prayer was
answered
by a young equestrian artist
who intended to draw a horse
on that very site.
A horse is no substitute for an
elephant,
But nothing is.

SPIKE MILLIGAN, 1999

Akukho ndlovu isindwa
    ngumboko wayo
No elephant is overburdened
    by its own trunk

From XHOSA PROVERBS
by Zolile Calana, Kwela Books, 2002

Contents

1 Introduction: Reformation and Pragmagic

As we write this introduction we are very conscious of magic. Magic, it seems, is a catchy theme right now, both in our own lives and in the world around us. This is hardly surprising, what with J. R. R. Tolkien's *Lord of the Rings* and J. K. Rowling's *Harry Potter* stories having come to life on the big silver screen. But the magic we are talking about is not of the wizardry kind. Merlin can stay in his cave. Nor is it of the David Copperfield genre where the audience knows that they're being hoodwinked but are prepared to suspend their belief in the interests of excitement. No, we are talking about something more genuine, more tangible, more practical – what brain-mind researcher Marilyn Ferguson called 'pragmagic'.

In our interpretation of the word, magic is the revelation that results from a profound change in perception or understanding. The superstitious world of the Middle Ages was magically transformed by the wizards of art and science – Da Vinci, Galileo, Copernicus and Newton. Then the quantum physicists waved their wands and subtly altered Newton's clockwork universe. Today, the magic continues as the seemingly impossible is conjured up with breakthroughs in areas like biotechnology, artificial intelligence and human consciousness.

But magic is not restricted to the sciences. Nelson Mandela and F. W. de Klerk wove their own form of magic to create the New South Africa. Unlike in art and the sciences where the magic is normally provided by individuals working on their own, the magic in politics often comes from the development of a positive chemistry between the leading players. This chemistry then leads to an outcome greater than the contribution of any individual member and takes them all by surprise.

Nevertheless, as with everything in life, there's good magic and bad magic. The swastika was bad magic. When Hitler unfurled it, he temporarily turned the most scientifically advanced nation on Earth back into savage barbarians. In his footsteps followed Stalin, Mao and Pol Pot, who turned their followers into killing machines of their own people. By the millions. And the chemistry was pure evil. Today bad magic continues to bedevil regions like the Middle East and Northern Ireland where thirst for revenge plunges ordinary people into acts of lunacy and callousness. In the name of God or Allah. And He is always on *your* side.

What, you may be asking, has all this to do with business? Well, magic has everything to do with business and this book. For the simple reason that bad magic has moved many companies into a state that is beyond reasonable greed. And the public have a good idea of the boundary between 'reasonable' and 'obscene'. Recently in South Africa, we have had several disclosures on the size of individual packages and the terms of share incentive schemes which have caused enormous outcries. They have been clearly out of whack with the norm. To give the companies concerned the benefit of the doubt, they may not have consciously exceeded the limits of reasonableness. Their boards probably comprise the normal spectrum of saints and sinners; but somehow they have allowed themselves to be collectively swept along by the prevailing paradigm of success which is purely financial, and that in turn has led to unreasonable behaviour. In light of Enron's failure, this judgement may be overly kind and more cases of dodgy accounting, inflated profits and insider trading by the board may pop up in Corporate America and Corporate Europe. Unreasonable greed never lies far below the surface – not even in the public at large. That's why national lotteries have such an immense first prize rather than a more even sharing of the winnings. People are mesmerised by extraterrestrial sums of money. So we want to break the spell. We want to indulge in good magic by challenging and changing the orthodox perceptions surrounding business – making the chief executive officers (CEOs) realise the limitations of their current modes of understanding and habits of practice. Above all, we want to persuade them to let go of their conditioning just long enough to glimpse a fantastic new vision of what business could be in the twenty-first century.

Bluntly put, we are seeking a reformation in business along the same lines as the one precipitated by Martin Luther in 1517. On October 31 of that year, he wrote an attack on the sale of indulgences (remissions of punishment for sin) in 95 theses which he nailed to a church door. His basic point was that the Church had become too interested in enriching itself at the expense of its true mission of providing spiritual leadership. It had lost the support of the population at large with its mercenary practices and obsession with grandeur and wealth. In exactly the same way, the modern corporate world has lost the confidence of the person in the street. The high priests of business – the board of directors – are perceived as just another example of a group of privileged people driven by unreasonable greed and feathering their own nests. The customers and shareholders come a poor second and other stakeholders trail even further behind. The modern equivalent of indulgences is an astronomical salary, a large wad of share options and a corporate jet. And the modern equivalent of the flowery and unintelligible prayers which the Church used to recite in order to extract its indulgences from the peasantry is the purple prose and lofty sentiments expressed by companies in their mission statement, combined with a set of accounts that only the initiated can understand.

The other high-sounding phrase that has been introduced into the boardroom is corporate governance. But if the unfolding Enron saga is disclosing anything, it is that corporate governance is sometimes not worth the (shredded) paper it is written on – and, boy, is there plenty of paper! Should the people involved in implementing corporate governance not have their hearts in the right place and just be going through the motions, the process becomes a charade.

You can have all the nonexecutive chairpersons, nonexecutive directors, remuneration committees, audit committees, environment, health and safety committees and external auditors you like, but things will go hideously wrong if ceremony has replaced substance and cynicism is the order of the day. Some nonexecutive directors sit on so many boards that it is physically impossible for them to exercise their fiduciary responsibilities properly. Worse still is a situation where the chairman and the CEO are one and the same person and he has managed to load the board with his buddies. If things go right, they are the first to congratulate him and approve a handsome bonus. If things go wrong, they are the last to ask the tough questions needed to expose malpractice. They would prefer to have the wool pulled firmly over their eyes even though ignorance is no excuse in terms of the law. At least the Enron saga will mean that shareholders will no longer rubber-stamp the appointment of external auditors and nonexecutive directors. They will want them as *real* representatives to monitor what management is doing. But as we shall argue later on, we believe that this representation should be extended to other types of stakeholders as well.

So reform is critical for business to restore its reputation, particularly as its presence in society rivals that of the Church in the sixteenth century. Hence we see business as establishing a new and broader role model, in keeping with modern times, rather than going back to the old one. Another word for this type of change is *shapeshifting* – liberating ourselves from the old form that defined and constrained us in the past and morphing into a completely new being, with new characteristics and potential for the future. The catalyst to which we refer often in this book and which will assist us in the process of shapeshifting is *sustainability*. Unfortunately, the word is almost a cliché now; but the idea behind it remains a powerful source of inspiration and is responsible for an umbrella movement encompassing as diverse a group as you can imagine – academics, avant-garde entrepreneurs, mother-earthers, pop singers, students, housewives, activists in nongovernmental organisations (NGOs), organic farmers, green scientists, politicians, etc. They all share one thing in common: an interest in improving human wellbeing by seeking a proper balance between social, economic and environmental change. Of course, the position of the fulcrum on which these three fields should be balanced differs considerably from person to person.

More than this, however, sustainability is a new way of perceiving business – its purpose, its methods and its impacts. For those companies that can adapt and respond quickly and intelligently enough, there are new markets to capture and profits to be made. For those that are ill prepared, sustainability is going to become a significant financial burden, even a threat to corporate survival. In writing this book, therefore, we primarily have in mind people in business or people who are concerned about business – especially managers and professionals focused on improving

15

the performance of companies amidst the complexity of budget constraints, market pressures, customer demands, community needs and profit expectations. It is an attempt to help companies to change in preparation for a very different future.

The book, however, is not only about business putting its own house in order. It is about business embracing the concept of sustainability, whether for reasons of moral conviction, fashionableness, practical necessity, image burnishing or business opportunity. But the commitment must be there. In order for companies to make real progress towards sustainability, it is obligatory that a fundamental recognition occurs at some stage that we face a serious global crisis. The fact of the matter is that, apart from the bad magic of September 11, 2001, which has captured most of the public's attention, our lifestyles, our products and our business processes are unsustainable. Sooner or later, they will harm or even destroy us and those around us – our health, our social fabric and our natural ecosystems. We know this because it is happening already. This book is for companies that have the foresight and the courage to be part of the solution, rather than remain the problem. Nonetheless, we have things to say to the die-hards too. However unpleasant the advice may sound, it constitutes a warning which should be heeded by them.

The book begins by looking at the nature of evolutionary change and defining the process of shapeshifting. It goes on to its central message that business needs to reform itself by shedding the predatory nature of the *lion* and taking on the more harmonious and compassionate character of the *elephant*. We then trace the history of sustainability from the original pioneers of the concept to the present, emphasising that sustainability is only possible if every level of society participates in the shapeshifting process. Arising from this, we seek to explain – by comparing the old paradigm with the new one – how companies and economies can *really* become sustainable. In the last chapter, we offer contrasting 'lion' and 'elephant' scenarios for the future of the world and outline the current options available to business. Finally, we make some practical recommendations on how CEOs – and all of us for that matter – can shapeshift: starting now.

So, welcome to the show. We invite you to pack your trunks and join us, as we try to spot what Destiny has up her sleeve. Eventually, we hope to persuade you to join us in starting a chain reaction where one day the international community will say: it's a miracle how business has turned its back on unreasonable greed. Mahatma Gandhi summed up our message better than we can: "The Earth has enough for everyone's need but not for everyone's greed." We want to prove that lions *can* change their manes even if leopards can't change their spots. The reason: pragmagic!

2 Evolution: Taken as a Whole

2.1 *Falling down a rabbit hole*

Being in business these days is a lot like falling down a rabbit hole. The latter, if you remember Lewis Carroll's classic *Alice's Adventures in Wonderland*, is a chaotic and confusing place to be. All the tried and tested rules of the past don't seem to work so well any more. The formerly familiar environment keeps transforming itself into new, unrecognisable landscapes. Strange, distracting characters have a habit of popping up randomly and then suddenly disappearing. And the clear, rational perspectives that used to spell out solutions keep getting stretched, warped and turned on their heads, like the reflected images in a house of weird mirrors.

It was not always this way. There was a time, not too long ago, when things were a lot simpler. Not necessarily easier, but clearer. Corporate leaders knew what was expected of them. The rules were unambiguous. Their job was to make more money for their shareholders. Success equated with a good return on investment. The challenge was in *how* to make more profits; *how* to beat the competition; and *how* to keep the customers coming back for more.

Ask any business executive if their world is still so clear. We have no doubt that they will admit to things being much fuzzier now. The demigod once known as the *shareholder* has mutated into a multiheaded beast called the *stakeholder*. *Accounting*, the time-honoured introspective discipline of counting beans (or gold or money or shares), has been turned inside out and become nerve-racking *accountability* to the big wide world out there. Arthur Anderson can testify to that in the wake of Enron's collapse. And *profitability*, which used to be a trustworthy financial measure, has multiplied into a *triple bottom line* by blurring together economic, social and environmental performance.

For Alice, as she meandered through Wonderland, a lot of the changes she had to cope with were related to size. She alternately shrank as small as a mouse and then grew as large as a house. As a result, she was forced to see the world through the eyes of the smaller creatures, as well as to realise her potentially destructive impact as a big, clumsy human. Also, in Wonderland, everything could talk – the white rabbit, the playing cards, the pipe-smoking caterpillar. Of course, the rules of the game were different as well. Croquet, for example, was played using flamingos as mallets and hedgehogs as balls.

In the topsy-turvy Business Wonderland of the twenty-first century, the changes also have to do with size, communication and different rules. Not only have some companies become as large and powerful as countries – Exxon Mobil's revenue in 2000 of $210 billion surpasses the gross domestic product of most of them – but the world has shrunk with the communications revolution. Suddenly, the formerly mute public citizen has an amplified voice through technology-enabled networking. The bark of a small NGO watchdog can resonate around the world. And the rules are changing at a dizzying speed – whether it is mushrooming e-commerce and free information, or rising expectations on corporate social, ethical and environmental responsibility.

2.2 *Avoiding the boiled frog syndrome*

In this bewildering commercial climate of whirlwind changes, it is not surprising that many companies operate on high alert and are permanently in an emergency response mode. They spend their corporate lives reacting to the latest crisis or opportunity – the quarterly results, the stock market fluctuation, the fiscal adjustment in the government's budget, the resource price, the technology upgrade, speculations in the media, the analyst's rating, the trade union's demand, the community's complaint, the factory accident, or the ecological disaster.

To some extent, business is just reflecting our natural human tendency to respond instinctively to obvious, dramatic changes in our environment. Like all animals, we are biologically programmed to react to visible, immediate danger through an in-built fight-or-flight mechanism. In this sense, we are well suited to deal with crises like war or catastrophe. Perhaps it is not surprising, therefore, that our Western corporate culture is saturated with military jargon – we formulate strategies, fight the competition, deploy sales forces, target customers, launch products and employ marketing tactics.

Needless to say, for companies battling amidst this storm

of change, it is often difficult to see the wood for the trees – to stand back and take a more strategic, evolutionary perspective. In fact, metaphorically speaking, business in most cases cannot even distinguish between the passing hurricane (the short-term change) and the more fundamental change in the overall pattern of the climate (the long-term shift). And yet making this distinction is critical, since each scenario calls for a very different response. The hurricane requires swift, defensive action, while climate change demands a more significant shift in overall modus operandi.

When business fails to distinguish the long-term effects of gradual changes, it displays the classic 'boiled frog' syndrome. If a frog is placed in boiling water, it immediately jumps out (providing it is free to do so). However, if the water temperature is cool to begin with and then gradually increased, the frog fails to register any threat to its wellbeing and consequently allows itself to be literally boiled alive. Such a creeping sensation has recently been felt by asbestos mining and cigarette companies as their losses in court mount. By contrast, it is only the company that deliberately sensitises itself to these underlying systemic changes that will be sufficiently prepared in advance to cope with them.

There are many examples of threats that could boil the corporate toads: creeping income inequality; the spread of HIV/AIDS; marginalisation of certain regions from the world economy; the cancerous burden of Third World debt; alienation of people with low incomes or no jobs; accelerating biodiversity loss; global climate change; rising chemical concentrations in the earth's water systems; disintegration of cultural identities; the spread of violent crime among the youth; the breakdown of the nuclear family unit; the risk of executive kidnapping, anthrax-laced letters and computer viruses, to mention but a few.

It is the contention of this book that most companies are

already in hot water (perhaps mistaking the cooking pot for a jacuzzi?). They do not recognise that the rules of the game are changing in radical ways that will soon make their cherished business thinking and practices obsolete. And they do not understand, or perhaps they have been too busy fighting shareholder-value fires to realise, that some of the imminent evolutionary changes will make for a life-changing experience. Returning to the Enron debacle, you can bet the relationship between large companies and their auditors will now change forever. How many have woken up to that fact already? No doubt the slow ones will be surprised when their knee-jerk policy responses, procedural tinkering or technology-based solutions prove to be too little too late, only bumping them from the frying pan into the fire.

2.3 *Spotting the hundredth monkey*

The best chance for companies to survive an accumulation of changes to the environment is to develop a better understanding of how evolution itself works. The popular Darwinian notion of a slow, incremental process of continuous improvement by random trial and error is only partially accurate. Evolution also happens in great leaps of sudden transformation, so-called discontinuities.

Small changes have a cumulative effect so that when certain thresholds are reached, dramatic metamorphoses are triggered. As a mathematician would say, most systems go nonlinear at some specific tipping point. When they do, that final change does something to the system out of all proportion to its own significance. The famous example given is of the butterfly fluttering its wings and causing a typhoon on the other side of the Earth: the weather was so finely balanced! But what are some of the real watershed moments in evolutionary development? In technological evolution, we can think of the discovery of fire, the wheel, the steam engine, the computer and satellite communications. In socio-economic terms, perhaps it was the replacement of monarchy with democracy, the abolition of slavery and the persistence of free-market capitalism when challenged by communism. A more mundane but interesting example is the conversion of smoking from a social to an antisocial form of behaviour. In each case, a few people at first apply the new science or the new idea and change their social habits. For a time the new phenomenon grows slowly. Then, kaboom! it spreads like wildfire, leaping all barriers in its path. Epidemics break out the same way: they start slowly but when they round the bend to the steep side of the 'S' curve, watch out.

This kind of step-change is often called the hundredth monkey phenomenon. The term refers to an experiment whereby certain behaviours taught to a group of monkeys were, after a particular threshold number was reached, somehow rapidly adopted by other monkeys of that species, without them having had any instruction or contact with the original experimental sample. A similar phenomenon was observed and tracked in the spread of the self-taught ability to open milk bottle tops among blue tit birds in the UK in the 1930s and 1940s. Experiments involving foreign languages, Morse Code and the QWERTY keyboard have even suggested that this 'threshold' dynamic applies to people's ability to acquire new knowledge or learn new skills. The more people already know, the easier it is for the next generation of students to learn. Pioneering biologist Rupert Sheldrake calls this phenomenon *morphic resonance*.

The important thing is that the point of inflection, the so-called tipping point, is always a relatively small number – substantially less than the 50/50 that one might suppose is necessary to tip the scales. This notion of discontinuous change was the idea behind the important concepts of *criti-*

cal mass and *paradigm shifts,* which became popular catch-words in the 1980s and 1990s. Marilyn Ferguson, whom we previously mentioned, was one of the first to apply this insight to personal and social transformation. In her exhaustively researched book, *The Aquarian Conspiracy,* she mapped out growing evidence that our underlying pattern of beliefs is undergoing a fundamental change. Across diverse fields, from physics and biology to medicine and economics, our picture of the universe and society as a rational, mechanical construct is giving way to a new creative, holistic understanding.

The emergence of the corporate social responsibility and environmental movements over the past few decades, culminating in the slippery slogan of sustainability, is a prime example of the hundredth monkey phenomenon. When companies began to be challenged on social issues in the 1960s by the likes of consumer activist Ralph Nader in the United States, these concerns were treated by business as distractions from their main purpose of profit-making. Likewise, multinational companies saw environmental issues in the 1970s as unreasonable demands by crackpot 'greenies'. In those days, greenies were a red menace. However, environmental and social concerns have risen like a tide over the intervening decades so that, today, sustainability stands on the brink of transforming the underlying business model that has been so successful over the past few hundred years.

2.4 *Seeing the greater whole*

For a perspective on evolution which will help prepare business for the step-change coming down the track, we must surprisingly look back to 1926. It was then that South Africa's former Prime Minister, Jan Smuts, published his book *Holism and Evolution.* In this philosophical treatise Smuts draws on

Darwin's theory of evolution, Einstein's theory of relativity and his own insights to reach the conclusion that there is a common driving force in all creation and evolution – a golden thread for which he coined the term *holism*. When fully appreciated, holism is a revolutionary concept that is highly applicable to business: so bear with us as we spend just a little time here on the theory.

Holism, Smuts explained, is a fundamental tendency within Nature (including human society and its institutions) to form *wholes* of ever-greater synergy. Synergy is the now well-known concept of the whole being greater than the sum of the parts. What characterises these wholes is increasingly complex relationships between their diverse elements, resulting in progressively higher levels of intelligence and creativity. The relationships between things are therefore as important as the things in themselves. Smuts shows this tendency at work in the most basic mineral and chemical elements of nature through to the organisational levels of plants, animals and humans. Interestingly, the real creativity in Nature occurs where fields overlap – where the outer edges of different wholes mingle.

Subsequently, holism has formed a sound theoretical foundation for extensive work on the nature of organisation and organisational change by people like James Lovelock, Peter Russell, Fritjof Capra and Peter Senge. For example, James Lovelock – a NASA astronomical scientist – applied the principal of holism at a planetary level although he may not have read Smuts's book. Lovelock discovered that the Earth displays the very same characteristics that are found in living organisms. He named his theory the Gaia Hypothesis after the Greek goddess of the Earth, Gaia.

Physicist Peter Russell extended Lovelock's thinking to include the social sphere. He suggested that human intelligence acts like the 'global brain' of this living, self-regulating, self-sustaining Earth system, with our growing communication networks forming the nervous system. Fritjof Capra, also a physicist, synthesised these ideas of interaction and self-regulation into a 'living systems theory' which is applicable to various disciplines such as ecology, biology, medicine, physics and economics. For example, it is a well-known fact in quantum physics that what you see is what you get. Light is a wave when you look at it as a wave and a particle when you look at it as a particle. In other words, interaction between the observer and the object he or she is observing will determine the outcome of the experiment. Finally, Peter Senge, business professor at the Massachusetts Institute of Technology, applied living systems theory to business under the label of the 'learning organisation' in his book, *The Fifth Discipline*. Wise businesses understand that they not only impact on the external environment, but the external environment impacts on them. Only by gaining knowledge of the interactive process between the physical universe, the markets, the other players and your own self will you come up with anything approaching sensible decisions. And even then you may be wrong because you underestimated the complexity of the situation or misread the dependency of one variable on another.

Looking at the development of human society over the past few thousand years, and especially the last one hundred years, the tendency towards more complex relationships is clear. Our global village is criss-crossed by almost instantaneous communication networks as well as increasingly rapid transportation links. Moreover, it has common economic structures. Indeed, just using the term 'global village' to describe the world is testimony to our growing recognition of ourselves as an interconnected whole. The emergence of multinational companies, international financial markets and a global trading system is therefore a manifestation of holistic evolution in progress. The Euro is but the latest example of a new whole being formed. Time will tell whether it is a sustainable whole which passes all the tests of evolution at the political and economic level. For that to happen, the new whole must function as a result of the willing cooperation of all its parts or sub-wholes. In contrast, when an individual component operates myopically at the expense of others or the diversity of the original groupings is completely sacrificed, the integrity of the greater whole is jeopardised.

Unfortunately, in many countries and companies holism gets short shrift. As this book will argue, some strategies of global business and the rivalry between certain nations show more similarities to selfish cancer cells taking over a body than a synergistic higher-order organisational form.

2.5 Searching for a new symbol

Symbols are like stories. They are a powerful way to tug at people's emotions, stimulate their interest and tacitly get their loyal commitment to a particular idea or set of values. Symbols of religion, mascots of football teams, the secret signs of cults – they focus the energy of the group by instilling a special sense of belonging in each member. But that characteristic invites division and exclusivity, the very opposite of what we want to achieve as authors. So our symbol is going to have to be carefully chosen if we are to get the corporate sector to buy into a more inclusive model.

Our central argument in this book is that the current model driving business has outlived its usefulness. The symbols of earnings-per-share growth, capital appreciation of the share, return on capital employed, market capitalisation, economic value added, so beloved by CEOs, the financial media and market analysts alike, are beginning to look empty beside the clouds building up on the global horizon.

We have clear and present dangers in the economic, social and environmental spheres which are exerting enormous pressure on the existing mould. It therefore no longer fits. Just as aircraft cannot land if there is no airport traffic control, the world cannot function if everybody is blindly pursuing his or her self-interest and there are no other rules of the game to ensure that the system as a whole remains intact. We are one world and business can react in two ways. It can either try to strengthen the present mould, perhaps by tinkering with its design a little to accommodate the stresses and strains in a better fashion. Trading in emission permits, which we deal with later, falls into this category. Even this is too much for the die-hard proponents of the old maxims like 'the business of business is business' and 'unrestricted free markets automatically ensure the greatest public good'. Any fractional deviation from such philosophy is pounced upon by these purists as a 'fatal conceit', to use the phrase of their champion, Friedrich Hayek.

Alternatively, business can search for a new mould, one that will make for a more comfortable fit with the new realities that are emerging. At the moment, the outlines of that fresh mould are still shrouded in mist, so it needs a new symbol around which it can take shape. The symbol indeed must be powerful enough to change the value systems of business people – especially hardened CEOs – so that they make decisions and behave in a different way, but on a voluntary basis. We certainly do not believe in a return to the type of society where such behavioural change is forced upon people by central planning or heavy state intervention. Be that as it may, we've already given you a sneak preview in the introduction of what our symbol is to be: an animal with no predatory instincts and, despite its size, a natural empathy for all creatures great and small. Such is the stuff of sustainability for the animal kingdom as a whole – and such is the stuff for those of us who roam the plains of business.

2.6 *Shapeshifting our beliefs*

Each time the world changes – when civilisations rise and fall, when new scientific theories challenge our understanding of the universe, when technological innovation reinvents our lifestyle, when political revolution breaks down the old structures of society, or when a global crisis threatens to destroy our planet – humanity is forced to let go of some of its most cherished beliefs in order to create a new mythology to guide its collective psyche.

We are living through such a time of profound change, and no more so than in the business arena. The old ways, which have dominated for the past century or more, are no longer appropriate for a postindustrial, sustainability-driven society. Sustainability is not only a new scientific, political, social and legal concept, but an entirely new business philosophy based on a new mythology. It requires that business thinks differently about its role in society and how it goes about what it does.

The changes needed in order for business to survive and thrive in an age of sustainability are so fundamental that they are akin to changing its identity, its underlying nature. At the moment, we believe that the majority of businesses embody the characteristics of a lion – an impressive predator. However, the future calls for different strengths, such as those displayed by the mighty elephant – a wise leader. Consequently the question is a simple one: how will today's lion companies change into tomorrow's elephant companies? Answer: they will need to shapeshift.

Shapeshifting is a magical or spiritual phenomenon contained in the beliefs of many of the world's ancient cultures and indigenous peoples. It refers to the ability of ancestors, gods, animals and gifted humans to change their form and take on the shape or the characteristics of a particular animal, often the totem of their particular tribe. Sometimes, this shapeshifting occurs to avoid imminent danger, or to ensure survival in the face of catastrophic change; at other times its purpose is to pass on special instructions for success or to impart timely knowledge and wisdom about life.

Faced with all the changes and challenges which the twenty-first century will bring, the knowledge and skill of shapeshifting is going to be indispensable to companies. This is not a new idea. A number of corporate shamans have admonished business to begin shapeshifting. Each of these soothsayers chooses his or her own mode of transformation, based on the particular vision of the future which that individual has. For example, one of us advised that companies should change from being bureaucratic hedgehogs into entrepreneurial foxes. The vision of the future driving this particular transformation was that of a world changing so fast that only an animal with the adaptability, resourcefulness and radar system of a fox could survive.

The image that fills the lens of this book's magnifying glass is one of sustainability, a world in which business is required to balance and integrate its economic, social and environmental goals – as well as its impacts. This balancing act is not just a dry policy statement made by the directors in the annual report or some glossy brochure. It is a passionately embraced philosophy that infuses every level of management and every action that the company takes. It lives! Shortly, we shall look at why corporate lions are ill-suited to respond to this challenge, and why elephant companies will be the new leaders.

Inevitably, this book will challenge long-held beliefs and uncover hidden prejudices. One of these, which we'd like to deal with upfront, is any prejudice people might have against elephants. That may sound strange, but what we mean is this. In Western culture particularly, elephants have acquired various negative associations. If these are not recognised and laid aside, the metaphor chosen for this book will be undermined – unfairly we believe.

The first and most important issue is size. Elephants are commonly seen as representing bigness, but in the worst possible way. For many people, elephants conjure up words like 'oversized', 'clumsy', 'lumbering', 'slow' and 'dim-witted'. Disney's Dumbo comes to mind. Obviously, these characteristics are not on the most-desired list for any business (or in choosing a spouse!). Nor are we suggesting, by selecting the elephant as a metaphor for sustainable business, that they should be. Certainly, we are not advocating that 'bigger is better'.

The elephant's size, however, does make it a relevant symbol of modern business. After all, there is nothing small about today's multinational companies. The critical issue is what they do with their immense size and power. As a point of fact, elephants do not fit any of the other descriptions given above. They are appropriately sized for their environment, extremely agile, one of the fastest land mammals, and one of the most intelligent creatures on the Earth.

A second commonly held stigma surrounding elephants has to do with their power or strength. They are often seen as overly destructive, aggressive or abusive. This, again, is certainly not the image that we are trying to convey about companies of the future. Precisely the opposite! But let us dispose of this perception very quickly. Elephants are only aggressive when they are threatened. For the most part, they are gentle giants that live in peaceful coexistence with all other animals. It is true that elephants can have a significant impact on the surrounding vegetation, but this is only problematic when their habitat range has been artificially confined (as is the case with wildlife reserves). Apart from this, the elephant's feeding habits are actually an aid to other creatures, making previously inaccessible vegetation accessible.

We find it a telling observation that it is mainly in the West that the elephant has a somewhat tarnished image, whereas it is a revered animal in the East. Interestingly enough, in the East and in Africa, elephants often have the same association with royalty that lions have enjoyed so strongly in the West. But more about the elephant's positive qualities later. We start our metaphorical story with a closer look at the lion's symbolic supremacy in modern business.

3 Conquest: The Legacy of the Lion

3.1 *The monarch on the throne*

The lion as an inspirational role model is neither new nor unique to business. Lions have won a place of respect and admiration in the imagination of humanity ever since we first encountered them. Their regal beauty, awesome strength, terrifying ferocity, efficiency as hunters and envied position at the top of the food chain have made them widespread icons for our own conquests and aspirations. Witness how many royal crests and emblems proudly display the lion as their symbol of strength and courage and how many kings have adopted Leo as their name. Take Richard I, king of England from 1189 to 1199, who spent most of his reign abroad fighting wars or as a prisoner. He became a hero with the public and was popularly known as Richard the

Lion-Heart. The lion as king also features prominently in the myths, legends, rituals and traditions of many of the ancient cultures of the world, from Europe to the East to Africa. In South Africa, the different words for lion – *ingonyama*, *ibhubesi* or *shumba* – tell us that it is a 'master of all flesh', one who 'makes the final decision' and 'the royal beast'.

Beyond its connotations of leadership and power, the lion is also the archetype for the popular 'survival of the fittest' maxim – the idea that Nature is a competitive eat-or-be-eaten world ruled by the 'law of tooth and claw'. Each creature has its place in the great food chain and will, sooner or later, be consumed by a predator higher up the chain: except for the supreme predators like the lion. Over the past few hundred years, this jungle metaphor probably seemed quite appropriate to the acquisitive rulers of the colonial empires. No less so for the people whose lives were dominated by the supreme rule of monarchs or dictators, and who were resigned to fighting wars and the daily struggle for basic survival.

More recently, the metaphor was found to apply with equal comfort in the increasingly competitive markets of the business world. As military jargon crept into the boardroom – strategy, tactics, targeting, etc. – so did the persona of the predator. After all, business seems to mirror the hunting instinct in so many ways. Competitors are chasing the same food (customers, new products, good talent, information, new markets and investors' capital) in a cut-throat environment of starvation (bankruptcy) or consumption (takeover of another company or somebody else's market). In this deadly game, it is seen as not only acceptable but essential to be selfish, ruthless and focused only on the prey. After all, those that are not hunting are soon likely to end up as someone else's lunch.

This view of the world is widely accepted in business, whether consciously or subconsciously. Its essence is found in a slight adaptation of a biblical quote: "Blessed are the meek, for they shall inherit the Earth – but not the mineral rights!" A recent article in *The Spectator* by Frank Johnson had the title 'Napoleon and Hitler would have been hopeless at business; so why is business obsessed with war?' It seems from the article that loads of executives read Sun Tzu's *Art of War* (c. 500 B.C.) in their spare time. Equally, everywhere you go in the office, you will run across corporate aspirations to display lion-like characteristics. Company pep talks and motivational seminars have all the telltale language – be agile, lean and mean, learn to hunt in packs, take down the opposition, get wind of what the competitors are doing, select your target market, keep your customers in sight, chase down business opportunities, go for the kill in the sales pitch. Jack Welch of General Electric is probably the most popular and revered CEO of all time. He sounds just like a five-star US General when he tells his life story 'from the gut'. One excerpt from his autobiography goes: "In those days, I was throwing hand grenades trying to blow up traditions and rituals that I felt held us back." His most famous dictum was that each of his divisions should be No. 1 or No. 2 in its respective market. Otherwise, it should be fixed, sold or closed. Period.

Such abrupt advice may have been fairly appropriate when the role of business was unambiguous – to make profits for the company's managers, owners and other shareholders. The consensus philosophy was to feed the pride and let everyone else fend for themselves. But the role of business is changing and the hunting lifestyle is proving to have a number of weaknesses in the new landscape of sustainability. The modern capitalist company, while it continues to portray itself as a lion king, has a number of blind spots with reference to sustainability. These fatal flaws or false assumptions that are beginning to challenge the supremacy of this kind of regal thinking are briefly discussed below. Before moving on, however, we must stress one thing. Our comments in no way pertain to that splendid institution called the 'Lions Club' which like Rotary and others does magnificent social work. Indeed, these 'Lions' are just exemplary elephants using an alias to conceal their good deeds!

3.2 *Master and servant*

"Some say eat or be eaten; some say, live and let live. But all are agreed, as we join the stampede, you should never take more than you need – in the Circle of Life". These lyrics by Tim Rice from the soundtrack of Disney's animated film, *The Lion King*, hit the nail on the head. Indeed, if a lion knows its place in the greater scheme of things, all is well. But when the lion's arrogance deludes him into thinking that he is better than other animals, his needs are more important and he can rule over his subjects like a dictator wielding pure brute force and fear, the Circle of Life is broken.

This latter scenario is, sadly, a fitting metaphor for modern business. As the nations and populations of the world have become increasingly tied into the capitalist economy, they have also become more dependent on its main agent – business. Business in turn has grown in size and power, until today it is the most influential organisation in our global society. This might have been all well and good if business acted like *Mufasa*, the wise lion ruler in *The Lion King*. Unfortunately, however, many companies are more like his ambitious brother, *Scar*, whose dangerous combination of power and lack of accountability turned his once lush kingdom into a desolate wasteland – echoing with the haunting cackle of hyenas.

People in business may think this analogy is rather unfair and dramatic. And to some extent, they may be right. The highly irresponsible Scar-like companies are perhaps few and far between. But if we examine the underlying pattern of thinking in business, there is a more subtle and insidious tendency at work. Companies constantly shrug off their social and environmental impacts because their economic contribution and financial profit are seen as more important; in fact, the latter are seen as an end in themselves. Companies are quick to point out how many jobs they create, what foreign exchange they earn through exports and how their continued success will trickle down to benefit everyone. Their beguiling argument therefore is that by enriching themselves, the whole kingdom is better off. There is no shortage of examples of this biased rationale. Pharmaceutical companies are allowed to price life-saving drugs well beyond the reach of the average sufferer in the Third World. The justification: they need to recover their research and development costs. Oil and energy companies refuse to 'give up smoking' because the upgrade of their polluting processes would damage their profits and hurt the economy. Hence, they continue to exacerbate global climate change and the health of the communities surrounding their operations. Logging companies clear-cut vast tracts of indigenous forest, emphasising the contribution of their sales to exports. Meanwhile, the world is losing irreplaceable carbon sinks and reservoirs of biodiversity.

The list goes on and on, each flawed decision accompanied by a plausible excuse. Fishing companies systematically deplete the fishing stocks of the oceans, but justify their actions in terms of contributing to the food supply and creating (short-term) jobs. Mining companies intrude on ecologically sensitive sites, but are allowed to continue because their operations boost the economies of marginalised communities or nations. At the end of the mine's life, they are seldom asked to make up for the *social* impacts that result from their withdrawal. Farmers are permitted (or even encouraged) to use chemical fertilisers and pesticides to improve annual yields, despite steadily rising contamination in the natural water system.

Sometimes governments and other worthy institutions actively assist in the perpetration of these unsavoury practices. For instance, the authorities might turn a blind eye to the effects of pollution on local communities because the industrial companies concerned pay significant rates and taxes. Arms companies are encouraged to export military equipment to support regional wars in distant lands because it will bring in foreign exchange. Local communities are incentivised to convert tropical rain forests into cash crops because this will help the country to meet its debt-linked structural adjustment conditions imposed by the World Bank or International Monetary Fund.

Obviously we are simplifying the situation and there are world-class companies who are notable exceptions. For example, Boehringer-Ingelheim has made an offer to the developing world to supply free Nevirapine for five years to stop mother-to-child HIV transmission. BP and BMW in South Africa and Debswana, the diamond mining giant in Botswana, have all set up HIV treatment programmes which include antiretroviral therapy for their HIV-positive employees and some or all of their families. Despite their profitability, Levi Strauss withdrew its operations from China so that it was not tacitly supporting the poor human rights track record of that country. And on the environmental front, Swedish furniture manufacturer IKEA supplied 532 000 low-energy light bulbs for free to the Swedish population in a campaign to improve environmental awareness and energy efficiency.

These are examples of companies taking decisions that

did not make short-term economic sense, but were in the interests of sustainability and long-term financial profitability. For the majority of companies, however, the belief pattern is clear. Business has become used to viewing its economic contribution (profits, foreign exchange earnings, jobs) as a justifiable end in its own right, irrespective of what social or environmental side effects it might cause in pursuit of this definition of success. The tragedy is that our current political and economic system perpetuates this back-to-front power relationship and makes it virtually impossible for governments, civil society or business itself to reverse the roles. This is akin to the lion believing that other species and the environment exist purely for its own gratification, which is neither true nor sustainable.

3.3 *An insatiable appetite*

This fatal flaw deals with business's unsustainable exploitation of the environment. All companies rely on natural resources and Nature's processes to some extent, whether as a source of raw materials, a factor of production, or a sink for its wastes. However, business has been extracting resources and impacting the environment at a rate and a scale that could only be sustainable if the planet were infinite and contained ecosystems that were able to regenerate themselves rapidly, irrespective of the damage they incurred – which is not the case. A few statistics illustrate the point.

The fossil record indicates that Earth has experienced five mass extinctions of species in the past 500 million years; in each case, at least half of the species in existence at the time were wiped out. Furthermore, after each extinction, it took between 10 million and 100 million years to recover former biological diversity levels. Some time in the past thousand years (probably in the past hundred years), the biodiversity of species on Earth once again began to decline, this time caused by human degradation and destruction of the natural habitat. We are precipitating what could rapidly become the sixth mass extinction. According to the landmark scientific book *A Walk Through Time, From Stardust to Us: The Evolution of Life on Earth,* we are losing an estimated three or more species an hour, a rate one hundred to one thousand times greater than the average over the preceding hundreds of millennia. And the trend is still accelerating.

We have lost over 10 per cent of the species that were living a few hundred years ago. Conservation biologists are predicting that half of the diversity of life will be lost in the next century if the present rates of habitat destruction and disturbance continue. In the last fifty years, according to the World Resources Institute, we have already lost, destroyed or seriously depleted two thirds of the world's agricultural land, half of the freshwater wetlands, mangrove swamps and rivers, a quarter of the marine fish stocks and one fifth of the forests.

Perhaps this is not surprising when one considers that, since 1980, the global economy has tripled in size and is expected to expand by a factor of five in the next fifty years, while the population has grown 30 per cent to six billion and is expected to reach nine billion by 2050. Or that world energy consumption rose from 207 quadrillion British thermal units (btus) in 1970 to 375 quadrillion btus in 1996 and is projected to reach 612 quadrillion btus in 2020. Or that the average of annual anthropogenetic carbon emissions, which was less than two billion tons between 1850 and 1950, has rocketed to 7.1 billion tons during the 1980s and will soar further to an expected 9.8 billion tons by 2020.

You do not have to be a genius to see that this trend is not sustainable. And yet most companies are still gearing up to continue their expansion, which will require additional exploitation of the environment and its resources. At most, an environmental impact assessment gets carried out, a few mitigation measures are recommended and the project goes ahead irrespective of damage. The problem, it seems, is that we have no mechanism to track and give feedback on collective and cumulative impacts. Each extra ton of pollution or waste may be relatively insignificant on its own, but it all adds up. How else are species lost if not through square-metre-by-square-metre of habitat encroachment? How else are communities disempowered if not by job-by-job lost?

Companies, and the governments that regulate them, do not seem to have either the will or the mechanisms to say "no" to new developments that deplete or harm the environment. No lion entertains the misguided belief that it has an unlimited food supply, so why do we?

3.4 *Pride and prejudice*

Physical growth is inherent in Nature, but it doesn't continue ad infinitum. How therefore can it be feasible for the lion to multiply at an exponential rate, or to consume more food each month, or to keep getting bigger each year? And yet there is a widely held belief that economic growth is always good and should be continuously striven for. At the heart of this assumption is the idea that if the economy is growing, everyone is becoming progressively better off. Wealth that is generated supposedly 'trickles down' through the society and the general standard of living is raised.

As a result of this thinking, politicians, multilateral agencies and economists point to gross domestic product (GDP) as the supreme measure of progress, welfare and quality of life for the nations of the world. It is the basis on which investment opportunities are assessed, development aid is granted, loan funding is allocated, membership of various political and economic 'clubs' is allowed, and general international status is accorded. This was never the intention.

GDP is a simple and useful measure of economic activity. As GDP's creator, Simon Kuznets, said in 1934: "The welfare of a nation can scarcely be inferred from a measurement of national income."

The evidence is beginning to bear out Kuznet's perspicacity. We know, for instance, that over the past fifty years, while the global economy has steadily grown, income inequality has increased. That is, the rich have become richer at a faster rate than the poor have become richer. Indeed, some of the poor have become poorer in terms of income per head. Furthermore, several indicators that adjust GDP for negative factors such as environmental degradation, poverty and health (for instance the Index for Sustainable Economic Welfare) show that, since the 1970s, our quality of life has been declining despite the increase in GDP. The United Nations' Human Development Index concludes that "the link between economic prosperity and human development is neither automatic nor obvious". In a similar vein, the World Economic Forum's Pilot Environmental Sustainability Index states that "there is no clear relationship between a country's observed economic growth rate and its environmental sustainability".

The United Nations Development Programme puts this qualitative difference in a nutshell when it identifies the following five damaging forms of growth: *jobless* – growth which does not translate into jobs; *voiceless* – growth which is not matched by the spread of democracy; *rootless* – growth which snuffs out separate cultural identity; *futureless* – growth which despoils the environment; and *ruthless* – growth where most of the benefits are seized by the rich. It has declared that these types of growth are "neither sustainable nor worth sustaining".

This is a fundamental challenge to one of the biggest myths of our time and one that pervades all business thinking – that growth is good and bigger is better. Now business has to face the fact that economic growth does not automatically benefit either society or the environment. And in the age of sustainability, where economic, social and environmental performance is linked, business will need to examine these relationships and impacts more carefully. When the lion pride grows, it may well be at the expense of other species and the environment.

3.5 Fat cats

Is the whole animal kingdom better off if the lions are getting fatter? Logic would dictate that, if anything, many species are probably worse off as the lions' appetite grows. And yet many companies claim and believe that society and the environment will automatically be better off if they simply focus on maximising value for their shareholders and increasing the packages of their directors. This conclusion is not supported by the dubious track record of business.

In lion companies, the benefits always seem to trickle upwards. Even employees do not seem to be guaranteed a fair share of the spoils, let alone society in general. According to the US Bureau of Labour, a typical factory worker received the paltry equivalent of 2.5 per cent of the CEO's salary in 1960. By 1990, this proportion had slipped to just 1.2 per cent. According to *Business Week*, US CEOs earn 85 times more than their employees and CEO pay increased by 92 per cent between 1990 and 1995 when it reached an average of $3.75 million per annum. During the same period, worker layoffs increased by 39 per cent. How can a more equitable world be achieved when, on the one hand, three billion people live on less than $2 a day, and on the other hand the wealthy have $8 trillion 'invested' in tax havens? To put this income gap into perspective, it would take one Haitian worker producing Disney clothes and dolls *166 years* to earn as much as Disney CEO Michael Eisner earns in *one day*. Across the Atlantic, *The Daily Telegraph* carries a story in virtually every edition of British CEOs playing catch-up with their American cousins in terms of stratospheric pay packages. A millionaire is now defined as a person who *earns* a million pounds a year! Rather than spreading around the wealth for the common good, it seems to us that Adam Smith's invisible hand has a compulsive habit of feeding itself.

Apart from the bizarre income gap between individuals that exists in the world today, there are too many examples to ignore of companies putting their own interests before the health and safety of their employees, before the welfare of local communities and before the integrity of the environment. Nike is found to be using sweatshops with child labour. Shell is accused of human rights and environmental abuses in Nigeria. Coca-Cola is put under the spotlight at the 2000 Olympics for still using ozone-damaging refrigeration. McDonald's is found to be farming beef on clear-cut tropical rainforest land. Tobacco companies are accused of including additives in their cigarettes to make nicotine more addictive. Internal e-mails between Microsoft's top management, disclosed in their recent court case, indicate a desire to dominate the market at any cost.

As most economists and business managers will tell you (if they are being honest rather than politically correct), the incentives in our current economic system make it almost impossible not to choose profits over people and the planet. Economists will talk about 'market failure', 'externalities' and the 'tragedy of the commons', while managers know that it comes down to social and environmental considerations simply being too costly in the face of unrelenting pressure from shareholders and others to make better returns and to achieve higher growth rates.

So, it is no longer appropriate to assume (if it ever was before) that bigger and more profitable companies are necessarily better for society, communities or the environment. At the same time, it is simplistic just to brand companies as villains without taking into account the economic system that shapes their behaviour. The relationship between how well a lion is eating and the health of its surroundings is neither simple nor direct.

3.6 *Is feline competition superior?*

This blind spot challenges business's assumptions about competition and its predatory nature. Companies tend to emphasise how creative they have to get and how keen their prices must be in a competitive environment. Yet the environment is seen as a resource to consume, customers are seen as prey to hunt down and other companies in the industry are seen as competing predators to be killed, chased away or consumed. But are society and the environment better off as a result? And is this the only model for corporate behaviour?

When thousands of staff are laid off, when knowledge is hoarded, or when an ecosystem is compromised in the name of competitiveness as happens regularly it is hard to argue that there has been a net sustainability benefit. And besides the social and environmental impacts, competitive behaviour may be inefficient in the long run. Take specialisation in agriculture. The world's range of crops and animals is narrowing due to dominant strains eliminating the weaker ones. More than 90 per cent of the world's food is derived from fewer than twenty species of plant. If the climate changes, it may be disastrous for agriculture as the new habitat may not suit the strains that are left. One of the reasons that Nature has been so resilient in the past has been its diversity and profusion which allow life to continue even when a step-change occurs in the environment. Nature really does abhor a vacuum! In our case, man-made competition has led to fewer options and less flexibility than the natural state. The same can happen in normal commercial markets when a big firm crowds out small firms. The end result is that the consumer has a more limited choice. Ultimately, he or she may pay a higher price for the product if the company left decides to exploit its dominant position.

To further our argument, consider this fictional illustration from Ancient Greece. Suppose there was a trireme race in the sea off the Athenian Coast to see which captain had the fastest warship. And suppose the speed of the trireme was related to how often the three rows of oarsmen were lashed with whips in each ship. Would you call the ship that crossed the line first the most successful competitor or would you say that it had the worst conditions of service? Yet this is precisely how companies vie with each other now. They bring in management consultants to cut headcount and costs to the bone, making the remaining staff work longer and longer hours. As a result, they may achieve market leadership and win the race – but at what human cost in terms of those that stay and those that go?

Extensive research by author Alfie Kohn also suggests that, in a business context, competitive behaviour undermines individual and group performance. On the other hand, a new breed of companies is emerging that emphasises co-operative relationships. Rosabeth Moss Kanter, former editor of *Harvard Business Review* and author of *When Giants Learn to Dance*, calls this becoming better PALs with other organisations – the new breed *pool* their resources, create opportunity-based *alliances* and *link* systems in a partnership.

It is all a question of emphasis. Until now, business has chosen to highlight and dramatise the predatory aspects in

Nature, whereas these are the exception rather than the rule. Nature's underlying characteristic is that of interdependent relationships and symbiotic cooperation. Even competition in Nature only takes place within a broader context of cooperation. Likewise, in a sustainability era, a company's success will depend on being able to cultivate win-win relationships with all its stakeholders. Eventually, therefore, the competitive lion will lose its throne to the co-operative elephant.

3.7 Living in a new landscape

The lion is a creature of the wide-open African plains. It thrives when it can roam freely over vast distances, hunting its prey without restriction. It will go wherever the food supply is plentiful, letting no animal stand in its way. It is as if the entire animal kingdom, and Nature itself, exists to serve him, to satisfy his hunger.

This is a fitting analogy for the way in which business has operated over the past few hundred years; roaming far and wide; ever hungry to conquer new markets; ever eager to track down fresh consumers; going where conditions best serve its appetite for profits, where taxes are most lenient, where skilled labour is cheapest and where environmental standards are lowest. This is typical of what economist Kenneth Boulding described in 1964 as the 'cowboy economy'. On the infinite plains of the cowboy economy, cowboy companies believe that there are no restrictions on growth, resource consumption or waste generation. They can live life recklessly in the pursuit of profits, gunning down whoever stands in their way.

But the landscape is changing. There are very few frontiers left to conquer. The world has become a smaller, fuller place, one in which the cowboy lifestyle is no longer appropriate. Selfish lone rangers have never been much good at building healthy communities where people agree to live by certain norms to ensure peace and shared prosperity. Nor is the Earth itself an infinite plain. The cowboys can no longer just move on to fairer pastures once they've exhausted the land where they are. After all, the pastures are under pressure from a growing population, and from the activities of other cowboys who may have already degraded the soil and poisoned the water.

Boulding talks about the need to replace the analogy of the cowboy economy with that of a 'spaceman economy'. The latter pictures the planet as a closed system which, other than the sun, has finite resource inputs and a limited sink capacity to absorb our wastes. It is an economy where material conservation, recycling and waste minimisation are paramount, since there is no 'away'. Bearing this out, the carbon dioxide concentration in the Earth's atmosphere is at its highest level in 160 000 years, having risen from 280 to 350 parts per million between 1850 and the early 1990s. That's one of the less quoted statistics about the Industrial Revolution. Svante Arrhenius was the first person to spot the link between this statistic and global warming in 1890. And we're still arguing over it! Another economist, Gareth Hardin, elaborated on Boulding's spaceship economy idea by introducing the notion of the 'tragedy of the commons'. Hardin demonstrated that, in any 'open access' resource system, the resource will be systematically depleted simply by each user acting rationally in his/her own self-interest.

Yet this is exactly what our modern economic and business systems, operating in the lion mode, are set up to do. Companies have no qualms about pursuing their own selfish interests (growth, profits, shareholder value), because they hope that somehow Adam Smith's 'invisible hand' will miraculously take care of the 'common good'. However, as we will show in subsequent chapters, the common good is not being served by today's predatory business model. Closer to the truth may be Hardin's melodramatic conclusion that "freedom of the commons brings ruin to all" and "ruin is the destination to which all men rush".

4 Caring: The Promise of the Elephant

4.1 *Trading in fangs for tusks*

The elephant is a truly remarkable creature, as literary tributes like *Elephants: A Cultural and Natural History*, which we have drawn from in doing research for this book, well testify. It is an animal that has been respected, revered and even worshipped in many of the world's cultures for thousands of years. While the Western world has been obsessed with the power symbol of the lion, the East has long held the elephant as its supreme animal icon.

In Hinduism, the oldest and most pervasive religion of the Indian subcontinent, elephants hold high status. In the original Creation, they are accorded the title of 'bearers and keepers of the universe'. Furthermore, one of the Hindu gods, Ganesh, who is the protector of wisdom, erudition and wellbeing, chooses the head of an elephant as his preferred form. Elephant legends also surround Guatama Siddhartha, the Buddha; some depicting the white elephant as the original carrier of his soul, while in others the elephant protects him from harm. Even today, Indian elephants are regarded as sacred, and many given a garland-laden funeral.

In India, elephants have also long been associated with kings. The book of Old Indian elephant lore states that "elephants are consubstantial with kings" and "the creator of the world created the regal elephant for the salvation of the world, and endowed him with majestic power and splendour". Elephants, placed on the same level as kings since ancient times, have therefore remained closely associated with India's rulers and their ceremonial occasions throughout history.

Of course, it is not just in the East that elephants have enjoyed special cultural and religious status. There is a particularly rich tradition of honouring the elephant in Africa. According to some traditions, elephants are reincarnations of gods who have been slain in the unseen land of the sky. Others believe that elephants live for hundreds of years and are reborn again and again in some magical way.

The association with political leadership is also strong. The iconic leader of the Zulu nation, Shaka, was called 'son of the elephant' and the king of the Swazi nation is still today known as 'the great elephant'. In praise songs, the elephant gets a series of impressive titles: 'animal of our kings', 'lord of the trees', 'master of the valleys', 'king of creation' and 'servant of the great Earth Mother'. There are also many African legends about the time before people lived on Earth, when all the animals of the bush lived together under one king – Elephant. The stories all describe this time as one of peace, justice and prosperity, for Elephant was a wise ruler. Lion made all kinds of attempts to become king, but no one took his efforts seriously. They all knew that it was Elephant who possessed all the qualities of genuine leadership.

One particular legend from Zimbabwe, recounted by Nick Reaves in *When Elephant Was King*, begins to hint at why the elephant is an appropriate symbol of leadership in the area of sustainability. One year in southern Africa, drought struck. The rains failed and the animals soon ran short of water. One by one, the water holes began to dry up and the animals' plight became very serious. Such was their distress that King Elephant called a council of all the animals where they were invited to come up with suggestions.

Having listened to their ideas, he decided that their short-term solution to the lack of drinking water was to dig a large, new well in the nearby river bed. The water table had dropped drastically and the animals had to work night and day without resting. King Elephant worked hardest of all, using his enormous tusks to dig deep into the river bed, while the others carried away the soil, mouthful by mouthful. Eventually Elephant reached water and the animals rejoiced, praising the strength and hard work of their wise king. Then Elephant made rules about the water hole so that the water should be shared equally and everyone could quench their thirst. He decided that the animals could only come and drink at sunrise and sunset.

That is only half of the story. Lion disobeyed the rules and crept down in the middle of the night to drink his fill. He also had a bath and muddied the water. Then, in an attempt to discredit Elephant and usurp his throne, he gathered up some mud and smeared it on sleeping Elephant's feet. Fortunately, Lion's plan was neither well thought out nor cleverly executed. Not only did he forget to clean the mud off of his own paws, but his tracks were the only fresh spoor at the water hole. Lion was banished from Elephant's kingdom and King Elephant retained the trust of his subjects and reigned over them for a long time. The rains returned and life was good.

The end of the story is also worth noting. By the time old Elephant died many years later, he was the most respected animal in the land. Lion now had his chance and proclaimed himself to be King of the Beasts. After his takeover many things changed and the animals of the bush were no longer ruled by a fair and just leader. There was much grumbling and you would often overhear statements such as: "If only things were like they used to be, when Elephant was King!"

What if, in business, Lion was no longer king? What if Elephant was king (or queen) once more? For, according to the theme of this book, in the corporate bushveld of the future where social equity and environmental sustainability are the watchwords of society, Elephant has all the right characteristics to be the leader.

4.2 *Masters of survival*

Elephants are the epitome of sustainability, having survived for fifty million years and having evolved through the forms of more than three hundred species to reach us today as our largest land mammal. They have shown themselves to be supreme survivors and masters at adapting to different regions, climates and habitats. From their origins on the dry, grassy plains of Africa, they spread across all the continents except for Australia, adjusting to steamy tropical rain forests, sandy coastal deserts, extreme mountain terrain and snowy temperate zones. They have even survived an ice age.

As with companies that wish to endure, adaptation is the key. The desert elephants have evolved into more slender creatures with longer legs to cope with the sandy conditions, while the forest varieties are smaller and more compact. The elephants also have the ability to modify their behaviour, depending on the prevailing circumstances. For example, during a drought, they are able to regulate their reproductiveness so as not to give birth to young when the chances of survival are poor. When they migrate during the dry season, they also break up into smaller groups to allow greater flexibility in the face of scarce resources.

Lion-like companies stand in marked contrast. Although proving themselves to be extremely innovative and flexible when dealing with highly visible threats constituting typical fight-or-flight situations, they have a very poor radar system when it comes to picking up and responding to more fundamental, invisible changes over long periods of time. After all, the modern capitalist corporation, especially the multinational, is for the most part less than a hundred years old and already it is threatening to destroy the very social and ecological fabric on which it depends. Companies are going to need to learn what it means to survive epochs and symbolic ice ages, and the elephant can lead the way.

4.3 Benefactors of cooperation

Elephants are not predators. They are complete vegetarians living from the land, not off their fellow-creatures. They have no natural enemies other than humans and are seldom seen in violent encounters with other species. In fact, bush lore has it that despite their tremendous size, elephants in the wild go out of their way not to harm any other animals in their path, no matter how small.

As a rule, the elephant's relationship to other species and Nature is highly cooperative and symbiotic. For example, elephants often provide the lifeline that other animals need in the dry bushveld by digging for water, or enlarging existing water holes. Their eating habits, which often appear destructive, simultaneously open up the forest canopy to allow young growth better access to the sunlight and make previously inaccessible vegetation more widely available to other species. They also fertilise and distribute the seeds of a large variety of plants, earning them the nickname of 'gardeners'. Not only are they the plumbers and gardeners of the wild, they are also the road-builders, leaving a vast network of trails that give other creatures pathways through sometimes dense habitat. Elephants' cooperation with humans is also legendary, from the storybook tales of Tarzan and Mowgli, to the real-life war elephants of Hannibal and the hardworking domesticated animals of India and Africa.

In the complex world of wider accountability to stake-holders, sustainable companies will need to learn to survive not by their ability to hunt and kill, but by their capacity to identify, nurture and sustain cooperative relationships. Like the elephant, this behaviour will be in spite of or perhaps even because of their great size and power in the modern world. Incidentally, America as the most powerful nation on Earth will need to take the same lesson to heart, having operated almost entirely in a lion-like mode since the terrorists struck in New York in September 2001. Interestingly, W. E. Gladstone's words in England during the second Afghan war in 1880 demonstrated that Britannia at the height of her imperial authority could still produce a prime minister with an elephant-leaning belief system. He said: "The sanctity of life in the hill villages of Afghanistan, among the winter snows, is as inviolable in the eyes of Almighty God, as can be your own." Do the present generation of Western lions honestly believe that Afghan lives are as precious as their own? We have our doubts, despite claims that everything was done to avoid 'collateral damage' during the bombing campaign in Afghanistan.

4.4 *Inspirers of greatness*

Elephants' awesome size and strength inspires respect and admiration from humans and other animals alike, although they do not abuse their power. While some of their ancestors stood an incredible 13 feet at the shoulder, a full-grown African elephant bull remains supremely impressive, measuring 11-12 feet at the shoulder and weighing around 6 tons. In terms of size and strength, the analogy with today's multinational corporations is a fitting one.

But it's not just that they are big; it's how elephants carry themselves that count. When they walk, there is a remarkable grace in their movement. When threatened, they can move quickly across the ground, reaching speeds of up to forty kilometres an hour. When stretching for food just out of reach, they show unbelievable balance and agility. When moving through the bush or forest, they can travel with great stealth and silence. In fact, the bone structure of their feet is designed so that they constantly walk on tiptoes, cushioned by a pad of fatty tissue across their soles. And when duelling for mating dominance, they give breathtaking displays of coordinated aggression like an intricate dance between highly trained warriors.

The key for sustainable companies is not only to learn to find this grace and flexibility despite their size, it is also to be creatures of inspiration. Like Dumbo, they need to believe they can fly against the odds and in the face of public perception. They need to add new symbols to the traditional symbols of success adored by fund managers, not for show but because it is the right thing to do. Above all, big business needs to exchange a reluctance to display generosity – because it is a sign of weakness to give anything away that you don't have to – for a more conscientious and caring image. They need to inspire smaller companies to follow in their footsteps.

4.5 Leaders of compassion

Elephant life in the herd is governed by a matriarch; in family and clan, all authority is vested in experienced mother elephants who demand respect and are acknowledged as the herd leaders. They alone protect and lead the growing calves; they maintain order and harmony in the groups; they face the foe with courage and aggression when danger threatens. The role of each cow in the herd is clearly defined, from the leader to the rear guard, in family groups that can number up to twenty or thirty animals.

This matriarchal social structure also appears to manifest

in the kind of values that dominate the herd. Relationships are paramount, constantly nurtured through communication and bonding. Caring for and protecting the next generation is every adult elephant's prime concern. And paying tribute to their deceased companions is a ritual of compassion that moves all who witness it. Elephants are known to linger over the carcasses of their dead, forming a laager to ward off the first waves of predators. Or when they encounter only the skeletal remains of another elephant, they can be seen gently touching and smelling the bones with their trunks, with some even carrying a bone with them for a while afterwards.

Achieving comparable levels of social cohesion, empowering women in leadership and embracing caring values and compassionate attributes – these will be the strengths that allow sustainable companies to survive and thrive in the new age of stakeholder-shaped management.

4.6 Champions of communication

Elephants possess highly developed senses that allow them to be in constant communication with their family and the larger herd, while simultaneously receiving information-laden feedback from the environment that surrounds them. An elephant's trunk, comprising more than ten thousand muscles and millions of nerves, is like an amazing multifunctional 'technology', capable of transmitting messages, picking up scented codes, gathering fuel, washing, not to mention caressing and playing. With this remarkable instrument, an elephant can smell water twelve miles away.

Elephants have a rich and varied language of communication and a range of sounds to express moods and feelings: a purring vibration denoting pleasure as they greet one of their kind; a rumbling sound in the throat when feeling pain; a soft, moaning squeal when experiencing loneliness and boredom in captivity; a hissing rumble of anger; and an eerie melodious 'singing' when in community. Their most incredible ability, however, was only discovered by American zoologist, Katherine Payne, in 1984 when she began to wonder why 'the air trembled' around elephants sometimes. Subsequent research has shown that elephants communicate with each other over vast distances using infrasound, namely frequencies that are too low for the human ear to hear.

Sustainable companies will likewise need to be geniuses of communication, using a wide variety of media channels to ensure that they are in tune with the needs and opinions of their stakeholders. They will need to improve their communication 'hardware' to ensure real-time monitoring of environmental impacts and have structured forums for receiving stakeholder feedback. Amazingly, CEOs on the whole spend very little time capturing relevant information about the external environment. They flick on CNN to watch the news headlines in the morning and skim through the newspapers over breakfast. The whole day is spent studying internal memoranda so that by the time they get home they're too tired to read or watch television. Like good lions, they go to sleep after the evening meal!

4.7 *Keepers of wisdom*

Elephants are among the most intelligent creatures in the world. With the largest brain of any land mammal and a brain-to-body mass ratio second only to humans, they also have among the highest 'intelligence index' of any animal: 104 compared, for example, with that of the dolphin at 121 and the human at 170 (we are not talking IQs!). The prolonged period of childhood shared by the elephant species is another indication of its evolutionary intelligence.

Elephants display a remarkable capacity for learning in captivity as well as in the wild. What's more, they seem to share acquired knowledge amongst themselves. For example, when one elephant in a group experiences the shock from an electrified fence, none of the others will touch the fence; somehow, they invisibly warn each other and learn from each other's mistakes.

There is also the legendary capacity that elephants have in terms of long-term memory; hence the saying 'an elephant never forgets'. Often, researchers or keepers have been recognised after decades of absence, with some elephants demonstrating their capacity for bearing a grudge. For example, after being tricked into eating some vile medicine by the keeper at the Dresden zoo in Germany, the African bull elephant Jumbo would vent anger at the keeper and refuse to let him approach, even pelting him with rocks when he spotted him at a distance. More than this, elephants appear capable of passing on their learning from one generation to another, as has been witnessed from certain behavioural responses of young elephants when culling has been reintroduced after a long moratorium.

For all these reasons, it is perhaps not surprising that elephants are associated with wisdom by many ancient cultures. Their life span is about sixty to seventy years, not much shorter than our own. Some African tribes even refer to their tusks as 'wisdom sticks'. Like the elephant, sustainable companies will need to be far more intelligent than today's lion-like companies. They will need to remember constantly why they changed to environmentally-friendly processes in their factories and plants; why they spend more time and money on social responsibility programmes than their competitors; why they allow their staff to lead more balanced lives with their families instead of making them work around the clock; and why they must never get too complacent with their success. In the end, they will be rewarded for never forgetting. As the nineteenth-century German philosopher Arthur Schopenhauer observed: "The idea of the elephant is imperishable".

5 Sustainability: Catalyst for Transformation

5.1 *The mammoth was not sustainable, but what is?*

Before exploring how sustainability will change economics and business, we need to understand what sustainability is and what it is not, and how it came about as a force in our society. Essentially, sustainability – the ability of something living to sustain itself – is about surviving over the long term. The mammoth was clearly not sustainable, although proboscideans (the elephant family) have arguably shown remarkably good sustainability, having evolved and survived over fifty million years.

Even more interesting is the way we refer to dinosaurs these days. They only come up in conversation when we are being disparaging about some organisation or other threatened with extinction. Yet, as a species they survived for 165 million years! In contrast, it is estimated that hominids have been around about five million years; and it is only five thousand years since Stonehenge was built by the Ancient Britons. We've come a long way in the blink of a geological eye. Do you think we are going to last the pace for another 160 million years? Or is the next intelligent species on Earth going to use us instead of dinosaurs as the example of what *not* to be if you want to survive?

You will infer from the previous paragraph that a fundamental assumption of this book is that sustainability is conspicuously absent from the present. It is stating the obvious, we know, but we would not be writing about sustainability if we (and many others) believed that our current situation *is* sustainable. Thus when we home in on a sustainable economy and sustainable companies of the future, we are also implying that current practices are *not* sustainable. So sustainability is not the status quo – it is not the economy of the lion, with lions as companies. Secondly, sustainability is not about infinity. If we ask, "can life on Earth be forever sustainable?", our present theories of the universe would suggest "no". Barring an intervening catastrophe like Earth being hit by a massive asteroid, life as we know it will cease to exist in a few billion years when the sun burns out. We probably cannot do much about it and, frankly, it is too far in the future for us to worry about.

So, that leaves us with sustainability somewhere between the present and a few billion years' time. Not helpful! So let's examine it from a different angle. Perhaps the time scale should depend on our human capacity to think ahead and to care about the future. Most of us struggle to think beyond our own lifetimes. At a stretch, we can take in those of our children or grandchildren as well. In business, we are much more short-sighted, living like slaves to this year's calendar, the next quarter's performance and this week's diary schedule. Even strategic planning seldom stretches beyond ten years. However, the real villain of the piece in business is a measure called the discount rate, whereby future revenues and costs are discounted at a certain rate on the grounds that money now is worth more than money in the future.

Many companies use a discount rate of around 20 per cent, which means that in ten years' time a benefit or a cost has to be divided by just over six to obtain its present value. So let's say you have a project which in ten years' time gives you a one-off estimated financial benefit of $6 million. If you spend more than $1 million now, you should not go ahead with the project, according to the logic being applied. If we increase the period before the benefit is felt to twenty or thirty years, you can't basically justify *any* expenditure in the current year. But it gets worse. Imagine a project with an environmental benefit, for example one that involves cutting back on carbon dioxide emissions. Apart from discounting the future benefit, many business executives will question the validity of the benefit itself since they entertain doubts about global warming. Moreover, even if they do believe in global warming, there are no simple models with which to calculate the benefit. Hence, the cost is certain, but the benefit is uncertain and cannot be quantified. You may remember Madonna singing: "We are living in a material world and I am a Material Girl". Most financial directors are material guys who like dealing with figures which have some degree of precision. Otherwise, they are not interested and will give the thumbs down. Bad luck for sustainability!

We know that it is this short-term, lion-like thinking that is partly to blame for today's social and environmental problems. So we have a dilemma. On the one hand, ecological sustainability demands that we look at periods of time for which the human mind is not wired. For example, biological diversity takes between 10 million and 100 million years to recover once lost. On the other hand, we have to encourage people to think considerably more long term than they do at the moment. The pragmatic answer is probably to test any project against the following criterion: over the next 50 to 100 years, according to the various indicators of sustainability (economic, social and ecological), do we expect the activity to make the situation worse? If the answer is yes, the activity is probably not sustainable and we should reject it.

So much for what sustainability is not. The rest of this chapter is about exploring what sustainability is. In order to do this, we have taken heed of the story about the fleas on the elephant. The supreme council of fleas sends out a message to all its subjects living on Planet Elephant to submit their description of the mighty elephant. A flea living on the elephant's leg replies that Elephant is fat and round like a huge tree. A flea living on the elephant's ear says that Elephant is flat and wide like a pancake. A flea living on the trunk describes Elephant as a massive rubbery hose-pipe, while a flea on its tail talks about a long, thin vine with bristles.

Of course, they are all partially right, but none of them is able to stand back and see the big picture – the whole elephant. We believe that it is probably the same with sustainability. There are a wide range of ideas and beliefs on the subject and rather than try to choose the correct one or the best one, the rest of this chapter puts forward a mosaic of these perspectives. With a bit of luck, by the end an impressionist painting of an elephant called Sustainability will emerge.

5.2 *The sustainability prophets*

Sustainability began as an ideological crusade about fifty years ago when a few voices in the wilderness gave a clarion call about how our civilisation was on a path to self-destruction. They were ignored as fringe fanatics or doomsayers. Nevertheless, many of these early sustainability prophets were scientists who had done their fair share of homework before shouting their apocalyptic warnings from the hilltops. In some ways, they remind us of John the Baptist.

Rachel Carson is widely regarded as one of the first sustainability prophets. In her 1962 masterpiece, *Silent Spring*, she argued that the proliferation of persistent chemicals building up in the environment was unsustainable for all life. Carson illustrated her case with the story of Clear Lake,

California, where residues of the poisonous insecticide DDT had accumulated initially in the plankton, then in the fish that ate the plankton, then in the water birds that ate the fish, at each stage increasing in concentration. The dead birds were eventually found with up to 1 600 parts per million (ppm) of DDD (a form of DDT), compared to the recommended safe concentration of 0.05 ppm.

Also in the 1960s, but concentrating more on social responsibility issues, was American consumer rights activist, Ralph Nader. One of Nader's first campaigns, published in his book *Unsafe at Any Speed*, was an exposé of the safety defects in General Motors' Chevrolet Corvair. The success of the book led to the establishment in 1969 of the Centre for the Study of Responsive Law (later nicknamed the 'Nader Raiders'), which began tackling ethical areas such as corruption in government agencies, the hazards of air pollution and lax regulation of the food industry. Hence, while Carson is credited with planting the seed for the environmental movement, Nader is hailed as sparking off the movement advocating that social responsibility as well as health and safety should figure at the top of the corporate agendas.

Among the other early prophets of elephant-like thinking in the 1960s, whose ideas have already been mentioned, were the economists Kenneth Boulding (cowboy versus spaceman economy) and Gareth Hardin (tragedy of the commons). In the 1970s, their ideas were substantially enhanced by the now famous work of E. F. Schumacher entitled *Small Is Beautiful: Economics as if People Mattered*. This was perhaps the first comprehensive critique of modern economics, argued in a language that both economists and lay people could understand. These sustainability prophets were the forerunners of a whole generation of disciples who will be mentioned in the next section.

In the same decade as Schumacher's work appeared, the sustainability prophets also started incorporating sociology and computer science into their critiques. One such was the study by Donella Meadows for the Club of Rome called *The Limits to Growth*. This highly controversial piece of research computer-modelled the effects of population growth, resource consumption and pollution over the next hundred years or so. Her findings showed an overshoot-and-collapse scenario for our human civilisation, a pattern which zoologists and biologists were already familiar with from studying the population dynamics of innumerable species. Many of her conclusions were questioned, such as the projection that food and commodity prices would rise over the remainder of the twentieth century due to impending shortages. In retrospect, these aspects of her model failed to materialise. On the other hand, her projections on rising pollution levels and population growth have been vindicated. Meanwhile, in 1992 Meadows wrote a follow-up book entitled *Beyond the Limits to Growth*, which showed that her conviction had deepened rather than weakened during the intervening twenty years.

Finally in the 1970s, as already mentioned, a groundbreaking elephant perspective was introduced to the public by James Lovelock. Lovelock had been working for NASA on a model to determine whether life could exist on Mars or not. In order to do this, he had to ask the question: what are the conditions which sustain life on Earth? But in the course of this investigation, an unexpected conclusion was reached. He discovered that the Earth, previously accepted by science to be an inert, physical object, appears to have the capacity to self-regulate innumerable conditions (for example, gas concentrations, climate and bacteria growth) in order to create a suitable environment for life to flourish. In effect, the Earth was displaying the very same characteristics as are found in living organisms. However, the system could be overloaded if humankind continued to dump waste products at the rate it was doing. The red lights were already flashing for Lovelock.

5.3 *Subsequent elephant pioneers*

The 1980s and 1990s saw a number of thoughtful leaders further the cause of the early sustainability prophets. Among them was a whole generation of new economists who questioned the sustainability of our prevailing economic theories and practices. The titles of some of their books give an insight into the challenging messages contained in their now classic works: Paul Ekins (*Wealth Beyond Measure*), James Robertson (*Future Wealth*), Hazel Henderson (*Paradigms in Progress: Life Beyond Economics*), Herman Daly (*For the Common Good*), Manfred Max-Neef (*Human Needs*). The common theme running through these books is that our current definition of wealth related to money is deficient; and therefore the science of economics – which is about the production and creation of wealth – needs fundamental revision.

Importantly, this growing clan of elephant economists led to the formation of The Other Economic Summit (TOES) in the 1980s, which sought to challenge the (then) G-7 Summit for ignoring social equity and ecological sustainability issues – especially as they pertained to the so-called G-77 countries or developing world. In the 1990s, TOES was converted into the New Economics Foundation in London, which now has various sister organisations around the world including the South African New Economics (SANE) Foundation. SANE has championed for some time the idea of a basic income grant to all citizens. This would inject money into many of the cashless and impoverished rural communities in South Africa and lead to the creation of a network of small enterprises in those areas. More will be said later on this subject.

A number of pioneering scientists have called for progress towards an elephant economy and business approach. We wish to draw attention to three of these: Amory B. Lovins, L. Hunter Lovins and Karl-Henrik Robèrt. Amory (physicist) and Hunter (sociologist, political scientist and barrister) are co-CEOs of the Rocky Mountain Institute, which they founded in 1982 to research innovative technological solutions to the world's social and environmental challenges. They are co-authors of the best-selling *Factor Four: Doubling Wealth, Halving Resource Use* (with Ernst von Weizsäcker) and *Natural Capitalism: The Next Industrial Revolution* (with Paul Hawken). They are widely regarded as the leaders of the eco-efficiency, cleaner production and eco-technologies movements.

Professor Karl-Henrik Robèrt, a cancer researcher and physician, has gone a long way towards describing the elephant. Robèrt started by trying to develop consensus on the scientific fundamentals, from which he then derived the four sustainability 'systems conditions' that have formed the basis of an international organisation and strategic framework called The Natural Step (TNS). The methodology and its application to business, which are described in a book entitled *The Natural Step for Business: Wealth, Ecology and the Evolutionary Corporation,* will be discussed shortly in the section on sustainability criteria.

Finally, there have been a number of influential business consulting pioneers, who have sought to translate elephant ideas into a vision of the sustainable economy and the sustainable company. The two we wish to highlight here are Paul Hawken and John Elkington. Hawken, formerly a businessman and now a full-time author/consultant, was one of the first to translate environmental challenges into the language of economics and commerce with his books *The Next Economy*, *Growing a Business*, *The Ecology of Commerce* and *Natural Capitalism: The Next Industrial Revolution* (with Amory B. Lovins and L. Hunter Lovins). His main theme has been that business and the economy should learn to mimic the intelligence of ecological systems which are not only more sustainable but highly efficient as well.

John Elkington, author and consultant, seems to have a knack for inventing new-wave business catchwords, having introduced companies to the notion of 'green capitalists' and 'green consumers' in two of his early books. More recently, he is the person who coined the term 'the triple bottom line', on which he elaborates in his 1997 book *Cannibals with Forks*. Elkington drew inspiration for his enigmatic book title from a question posed by Polish poet Stanislaw Lec: "Is it progress if a cannibal uses a fork?" In the wake of the greed-is-good 1980s, which were dominated by corporate mergers, acquisitions and takeovers, the cannibal metaphor as applied to business seemed quite fitting.

Elkington argued that, rather than expecting companies to change their dominant habits overnight, we should start by simply encouraging business to become more civilised, more sustainable. How? By using the three prongs of the sustainability fork, namely economic prosperity, environmental quality and social justice. Integrated and balanced performance across these three dimensions will become, Elkington argues, the new triple bottom line – the means and the ultimate measure of corporate success in the twenty-first century. This broad concept of sustainability has now been widely adopted in the business world and is also a theme running throughout this book.

5.4 *A herd on the move*

Reflecting back on the 1970s, it was thanks to the zealous efforts of the sustainability prophets that a new social phenomenon was born – the green movement. It was given a much-needed boost of credibility when the United Nations convened the World Commission on the Environment and Development in Stockholm in 1972 and published its World Conservation Strategy in 1980. Here was a new cause which young idealists and restless activists could get behind – the Earth and its most vulnerable citizens needed saving!

Throughout the 1970s, the movement was dominated by a wildlife conservation ethic. WWF, the World Wildlife Fund (now called the World Wide Fund For Nature) and Greenpeace embraced different tactics but essentially the same goal: to prevent the extinction of animals (especially cute and fluffy ones). The world was awash with campaigns – Save the Whales, Save the Rhinos, Save the Seals, etc. At around the same time, the International Union for the Conservation of Nature (IUCN) was focusing on establishing protected areas and the Convention on the International Trade in Endangered Species (CITES) was trying to tackle the economics of extinction.

However, with the spate of industrial accidents in the 1980s, from Bhopal and Love Canal to Chernobyl and Exxon Valdez, the spotlight began to shift from wildlife conservation to industrial pollution. Multinational companies were increasingly portrayed as the new poachers, the stereotypical lion predators. This coincided with the height of the Cold War and growing antinuclear sentiments among civil society and environmental activists. Many of the demonstrations that took place were nasty and confrontational, but remained isolated enough to be ignored by the broad spectrum of business. So long as environmentalists could be caricatured as irrational, emotional, hippie types, companies figured they could be easily discredited and would eventually go away.

It was not until the politicians were enticed into the debate that sustainability became a mainstream concern. This first started to happen in a big way in 1987, when the United Nations World Commission on the Environment and Development issued its Bruntland Report entitled *Our Common Future*. The report coined the term 'sustainable development' as: "Development which meets the needs of the present generation without compromising the ability for future generations to meet their needs." Some characteristics of the elephant are already evident in this definition, including social sensitivity and longer term thinking. However, the concept was crafted essentially as a political tool, tactfully allaying the fears of powerful business lobbies in the developed countries of the North by not being 'anti-economic growth'. At the same time, it soothed the governments and civic organisations of the developing world in the South by talking about development and intergenerational equity. It also befriended and found a guardian-for-life among the environmental pressure groups by putting their 'green' issues on the world map.

Five years later, in 1992, 178 country leaders paraded on the world stage at the United Nations Conference on the Environment and Development in Rio de Janeiro, more familiarly referred to as the 'Earth Summit'. The result was that nations signed up to a variety of conventions, agreements and programmes, ranging from climate change and desertification to deforestation and biodiversity, all aimed at making the now politically acceptable notion of sustainable development a reality. The Agenda 21 Program represented a synthesis of these commitments and has been a focal point for political action on the environment ever since. Progress achieved to date will be reassessed at the ten-year reunion conference, the World Summit on Sustainable Development or Rio+10 which will be held in Johannesburg in September 2002. It is expected to bring together over 50 000 delegates including 130 heads of state.

The corporate sector is not generally one to be caught napping, and the global gearing-up on sustainability issues proved no exception. In 1991, a group of fifty of the world's top executives formed the Business Council for Sustainable Development (BCSD) and issued its report entitled *Changing Course: A Global Business Perspective on Development and the Environment* to the 1992 Earth Summit. Pick 'n Pay's then chairman, Raymond Ackerman, was one of the contributors. Viewed in hindsight, this initiative smacks of 'lions in elephant drag' but it no doubt planted a seed of awareness regarding the need for business to shapeshift.

In a parallel initiative, the International Chamber of Commerce (ICC) launched its 16-principle Business Charter for Sustainable Development in 1991 and contributed a book to the Earth Summit entitled *From Ideas to Action: Business and Sustainable Development*. Today, there are more than 2 000 corporate signatories of the ICC Charter. Moreover, the World Business Council for Sustainable Development, which grew out of a merger between the BCSD and the World Industry Council for the Environment, has more than 120 international member companies.

Both of these business initiatives accepted the Bruntland definition of sustainable development. However, as the 1990s marched on and companies tried to turn the concept into action, it became obvious that the political definition was far too broad and vague to be useful as anything more than a public relations sound bite. If sustainability was going to be taken seriously by the private sector as something requiring implementation, more specific definitions were needed.

Finally, by the 1990s, it had become clear that the environmental and social movements were here to stay and getting stronger by the year. The last decade of the twentieth century saw the green trend being backed by politicians, consumers, religious groups, community organisations and business. Germany launched its Green Party; the *Green Consumer Guide* became a bestseller; liberation theology and feminism adopted convenient ecological arguments; and psychology began to explore the notion of 'deep ecology' as a spiritual experience. Improvements in environmental science and legislation helped to give the green movement teeth, while a plethora of internationally negotiated agreements lent the movement the popular legitimacy required to turn it into a mainstream lobbying group. Ultimately, business had little choice but to clamber on board and nail its green colours to the mast as well.

5.5 *Guides to elephant spotting*

Following the rise in political and social interest in sustainability, a few leading businesses have begun to question their lion persona and to wonder about the viability of a future as an elephant. Their criticism of the elephant movement, however, has always been that no one seems to agree on what an elephant looks like. In other words, most definitions, such as Bruntland's sustainable development and Elkington's triple bottom line, are too vague to be helpful when it comes to judging whether day-to-day business decisions are leading companies in the right direction or not.

For this reason, we are including here what we believe are a few of the more helpful attempts to develop sustainability criteria – guides to elephant spotting if you like. One of the simplest sets of environmental principles, which can be applied to business, was formulated by Paul Hawken as follows:

- *In Nature, all waste equals food.* In other words, the outputs of every economic or business process should serve as inputs to another process. Ideally, we should not be using materials that cannot be absorbed and used by other economic systems and ultimately by natural systems.
- *Nature runs off current solar income.* The sun's radiation is the only outside input to our closed Earth system. It is the only source of energy that (for all practical purposes) does not run down. Hence, in the long term, the economy should increasingly be fuelled by solar energy.
- *Nature depends on diversity.* The survival of all the Earth's living systems (including human society) relies on the existence of biological diversity. Biodiversity performs all of Nature's so-called 'free' services and should therefore not be compromised by business activities.

Former World Bank environmental economist, Herman Daly, followed a similar line of thinking, arguing that a sustainable society needs to meet three conditions:

- Its rates of use of renewable resources should not exceed their rates of regeneration;
- Its rates of use of nonrenewable resources should not exceed the rate at which sustainable renewable substitutes are developed; and
- Its rates of pollution emission should not exceed the assimilative capacity of the environment.

Karl-Henrik Robèrt, to whom we have already alluded, suggests that we go back to scientific fundamentals such as the fact that nothing disappears and everything disperses (the first and second laws of thermodynamics). Only the sun, via photosynthesis, increases the concentration and structure in matter that is consumed in the process of sustaining life. From these undisputed laws he then derived the four 'systems conditions' of The Natural Step, namely that:

- *Substances from the Earth's crust must not systematically increase in Nature.* This is because these substances (e.g. heavy metals), in sufficient concentrations, are harmful to organic life. And since everything disperses and nothing disappears, sooner or later harmful concentrations will be reached if substances are mined more quickly than they can break down in Nature.
- *Substances produced by society must not systematically increase in Nature.* This is because, once again, these substances (e.g. persistent chemicals), in sufficient concentrations, are harmful to organic life. In many cases, Nature cannot break these substances down into harmless components; or it cannot do this faster than they are being produced. In a few thousand years time, genealogists wanting to find out how we lived will find huge quantities of telephone directories and babies' nappies in our rubbish dumps if they ever excavate them!
- *The physical basis for the productivity and diversity of Nature must not be systematically degraded.* This is because life is sustained by a complex web of interdependent species and ecosystems which provide a wide array of 'free ecological services' (e.g. water purification, weather regulation and waste assimilation). Most of these services are either too complex or too expensive to replicate.
- *We must be efficient enough to meet basic human needs.* This is because humans are part of the environment and a key aspect of sustainability. Resource inefficiency, including inequities in resource distribution, not only obstructs a social system from becoming sustainable but also tends to compromise other systems as well.

You will notice that, except for the very last point, these three elephant-spotting sets of guidelines pass over the social dimension of sustainability. To a large extent, this reflects the general situation where much less work has been done on social sustainability, as it applies to business and the economy, than on the ecological aspects. At this stage, we would point mainly to the work of 'barefoot economist' and former business executive at Shell, Manfred Max-Neef. Max-Neef's framework on fundamental human needs stands, we believe, as the best set of social criteria against which one can measure corporate social performance.

Max-Neef's model identifies nine fundamental human needs that are common to all people, no matter what their culture or context. These are: *subsistence, protection, affection, understanding, participation, idleness, creation, identity* and *freedom*. These needs are not arranged in a simple ladder of priorities. Subsistence is obviously a requirement for human survival; but, other than this, they can be satisfied in virtually any order or in parallel. Sometimes they enhance one another; at other times they are in conflict. Also, although needs are fixed, 'satisfiers' – the ways in which people strive to meet their needs – *do* differ between people, between cultures and between groups. Companies who make their employees work excessive hours should note the inclusion of 'idleness' as a need! Indeed, the challenge for business is to check how its strategic decisions or significant actions affect the fundamental human needs of all its stakeholders in turn. Some pioneering work in this area is being done by the South African chapter of the organisation we referred to earlier in this chapter – The Natural Step. The authors of this new elephant-friendly approach, Peter Willis and Diane Salters, are looking to combine aspects of Max-Neef's model with the work of philosopher-psychologist Ken Wilber and The Natural Step framework. Their hope is to produce an integrated tool that business can use to test its overall sustainability, including the social dimension.

5.6 *Footprints of the elephant*

If they are handed an elephant-spotting guide, the first thing that lion companies ask is: what is the business case for sustainability? That's a bit like asking how the elephant hunts or catches her prey, which of course she doesn't. The whole essence of sustainability is that it is a wider view of business performance – beyond the tempting food of profits and revenue growth and shareholder value. Nevertheless, we have some sympathy with the corner from which lion companies are coming. And the fact of the matter is that, increasingly, there *is* a business case for sustainability, although probably not in as tangible a form as business executives would like.

In this section, therefore, we highlight some footprints of the elephant by listing ten elements of the business case for sustainability. Each of the summarised themes will be picked up again in later chapters. To the majority of these elements is attached an opportunity cost, meaning that companies which insist on clinging to their old lion ways will incur significant costs and lose ground to the early adopters of the new principles.

The ten elements are as follows:

■ *Sustainability extends stakeholder accountability*. Stakeholder groups have become powerful, well-organised agents in society, increasingly backed by the weight of the law, international NGO networks, public support and media interest. Lion companies will waste inordinate amounts of time, energy and money trying to manipulate or fight its stakeholders, while elephant companies will engage constructively with these groups.

- *Sustainability raises the bar of legislation.* In virtually every country in the world, as well as at an international level, legislation regulating environmental and social impacts is becoming more stringent. Lion companies will find themselves incurring significant fines, penalties and clean-up or compensation orders, as well as being targeted for litigation, while elephant companies will escape these costly outcomes.
- *Sustainability introduces new rules of trade.* Compliance with internationally recognised social and environmental standards is becoming a prerequisite for engaging in responsible global trade. Despite the counterproductive efforts of the World Trade Organisation, elephant-friendly countries and companies will increasingly refuse to trade with predatory companies who do not bear one or more approved marks of the elephant. For example, most large UK retail chains now do spot checks on the working conditions of their overseas suppliers.
- *Sustainability affects access to finance.* Since the financial services sector faces indirect risks from funding or investing in unsustainable companies or projects, banks and insurance companies will increasingly scrutinise their business partners and clients on sustainability criteria. Access to finance by lion companies will become more difficult and expensive, while financiers will actively seek to support elephant companies.
- *Sustainability affects costs and liabilities.* Dealing with corporate environmental and social impacts or infringements is becoming more expensive, taking the form of taxes, fines, penalties, legal costs, damage claims, clean-up costs and compensation payments. Ask Exxon, whose *Valdez* oil spill off Alaska cost them more than $8 billion. By avoiding these costs, and identifying savings opportunities through eco-efficiency, cleaner technology and

improved stakeholder relations, elephant companies will be more profitable than their lion counterparts.

- *Sustainability spawns new markets.* The switch to a sustainable economy will create new market opportunities in such areas as clean technology, ethical consumer products, ecotourism, sociocultural tourism and professional advisory services. Traditional exploitative markets of lion companies will decline, while elephant companies can invest in the growing markets surrounding sustainability.
- *Sustainability expands corporate governance.* All around the world, corporate governance codes, which are considered the ground rules for good business practice, are incorporating sustainability principles into their requirements for risk management, ethics and reporting on nonfinancial matters. Lion companies will more frequently fail the corporate governance acid test applied by stock exchanges, analysts and investors, while elephant companies will excel.
- *Sustainability quantifies external impacts.* Governments, using a variety of economic instruments such as taxes, subsidies and permits, are gradually forcing companies to reap the full cost or benefit of what they sow in terms of environmental and social impacts. Lion companies will be net payers due to their negative contribution, while elephant companies will be net receivers for their positive contribution.
- *Sustainability shapes public reputation.* Stakeholder support of companies will to a greater degree be influenced by their public reputation, with unsustainable companies suffering from consumer boycotts, civil lawsuits and disruptive NGO activism. The profitability and share prices of lion companies will be directly affected by repeated damage to their reputation, while elephant companies will attract loyal support.

■ *Sustainability influences investments.* Sustainability funds, which screen companies before purchasing their shares or investing in their projects, will more and more direct capital towards sustainable economic sectors and businesses. Lion companies will increasingly face questions by their stakeholders about their exclusion from sustainability funds and indexes, while elephant companies will obtain financial rewards and an enhanced reputation from their inclusion.

5.7 Multilevel shapeshifting

Business sector readers will be relieved to hear, and no doubt quick to agree, that the transition to a sustainable world is not solely in the hands of business. After all, business operates within the constraints of prevailing political, sociocultural and economic systems. And many of these systems are still dominated by lion-like tendencies. Not surprisingly, therefore, many corporate elephant wannabes are frustrated by the slow pace of change in their operating environment and the retarding effect that the forces of a lions' universe have on their progress.

For this reason, it is essential that shapeshifting towards sustainability occurs simultaneously at various levels within society. Individuals need to shift their attitudes and values. Customers must shift their consumption patterns and buying behaviour. Economists have to change their market theories. Business schools need to shift their view on what they teach and the importance of ethical topics. Governments must oversee a universal change in the rules of the game which has as its intended result a level international playing field. In short, multilevel shapeshifting has to occur. A lone elephant in a lion park has little chance of survival. Even in an ordinary game park, you only have to look at the bloody lessons of poaching. In one decade – the 'massacre' decade of the 1980s – between 50 000 and 100 000 of the peaceful pachyderms fell victim to slaughter by human predators. So elephants, big and strong as they are, need an elephant-friendly environment to survive and thrive.

Speaking of which, the most dramatic example of the necessity for multilevel shapeshifting is the HIV/AIDS pandemic in South Africa. No individual actor on the political or economic scene can turn this epidemic around. It will require shapeshifting from a 'denial' mode to a 'total onslaught' mode on the part of all parties at the same time – national and provincial government; local authorities and communities; the private sector; the trade union movement; schools and tertiary institutions; churches, NGOs and other elements of civil society generally; and last but not least, individuals. The holding of hands across all classes and colours of the rainbow, the sharing of the burden to stop the virus spreading and a concerted attempt to help the sick all imply a revolutionary attitudinal change. But it can be done if you recall the last words of the first chapter: pragmagic! Handled properly, HIV/AIDS could be the catalyst for transforming South Africa into a nation of elephants with a common enemy and a common purpose.

6 Sustainable Commerce:
Growing Tusks and a Trunk

So much for the background on sustainability and our earlier introduction to the metaphor of the lion and the elephant. In this chapter, we start going beyond the 'why' to the 'how' of sustainable business. We explore seven critical dimensions in which shapeshifting needs to occur in order to create sustainable companies. These are: values, vision, work, governance, relationships, communication and services.

So, if you're a lion, take a deep breath and don't pull your whiskers out!

6.1 *Values: It's in his kiss*

Values are exactly what they say they are – a reflection of the things we *value*. They are not motherhood and apple pie statements in annual reports, or candyfloss principles framed on the boardroom wall. If you want to know what values a lion lives by, the answer lies not in his well-groomed mane or his charming smile; as the rock 'n roll classic goes: "It's in his kiss!"

In other words, companies' values are betrayed by their actions, not their words or their spin doctor's marketing material. And an unreformed lion will never be a convincing elephant, no matter how real his mask looks or how much grey make-up he applies. It is only by behaving like an elephant, not by looking like one, that companies start to shapeshift. One of the authors watched a pride of lions at a waterhole in a Namibian game park as they refused to allow any other animal near it. The day was extremely hot, the animals were getting thirsty and tired. It was clear that the lions' intention was to weaken their potential prey to the point that they were much easier to catch later on. Perfectly logical for a predator, but not the behaviour of an elephant. It occurred to the observer that this scene perfectly mirrored the principle of exclusion widely prevalent in today's economies. As farmers merge and expand their farms to compete in current world markets, no longer being afforded the protection by the state they used to have, so less land is available for the smaller farmers. Of course, this exclusionary principle applies in any field where large companies are gobbling up the market by trading on their economies of scale. The end result is a small number of asset owners surrounded by a propertyless, unemployed, highly resentful proletariat. Have you heard that analysis before? It comes straight out of Karl Marx whose ideology these days it is politically incorrect to espouse.

While the previous paragraph would suggest that economies should become more inclusive to avoid a Marxist revolution, a lot of companies still embody values of exclusion. Why on earth have competition? Profit maximisation rests on domination and monopoly control. Hence, alive and well in a wide variety of 'mahogany rows' are the principles of self-preservation, paranoid secrecy, cold-blooded rationality, materialistic greed, egotistical empire building, distrustful stakeholder relationships, organised pack-hunting, strict don't-step-out-of-line hierarchies and inequitable class and gender divisions. This may sound overly like a Disney caricature of the evil antagonist. But if you step back and think about the corporate environment and the way in which managers behave and acquisitions happen, it starts to feel uncomfortably true. Don't get us wrong. We are *not* saying that business is the root of all evil, or that business people are devils in disguise. We are part of the scene ourselves. What we are saying is that the economy and business have adopted the lion persona so completely that the life of hunger and hunting and killing has come to feel perfectly natural. You see, the lion is not cruel; it is just being what it is – a carnivore. The difference is that business is not genetically programmed to be a predator. Neither are the people who make up companies.

Of course, many of those in control of pension funds and other investors argue that, given the current rules of the game, they want their investments to behave like carnivores because that way they get the best returns. They would be horrified if the CEO got up at an annual general meeting and announced that he was going to give half the growth in earnings towards fighting the war against

HIV/AIDS. Which is the reason that we made the point about multilevel shapeshifting. A lonely elephant has little if no chance of beating the lions, especially if the odds are stacked against her – though you will see later on in this chapter that we quote a Harvard study which claims the elephant can be victorious in the financial realm (as well as in all others) if the playing field is level. The tragedy is that most people spend their childhood being taught to become elephants – to be kind, considerate, gentle, generous, trusting, fair, friendly, selfless and cooperative. Then they get snatched away from their supportive family environment and find themselves in the clutches of a more ruthless master – the economy, the company, the boss, the bank. Very quickly, they unlearn their home-made values. They are taught to distrust their caring instincts and to forsake their former beliefs as feeble naivety. They are shown how dangerous and unfriendly the world is, full of hungry competitors and harsh conditions. They are bullied into 'getting tough' in order to survive.

In fact, we believe that most people, even people like General Electric's 'Neutron Jack' whom we quoted earlier, are elephants at heart. One thing Jack Welch did, which you simply don't see from other CEOs, was to send handwritten thank-you notes to his employees when he thought they'd done something special. Most CEOs only communicate with staff lower down if they're in for a roasting. Sadly, the majority of management take off their elephant masks as they leave home in the morning and put on their lion masks. It may not feel natural or comfortable; but it is expected. When in lion country, pretend to be a lion or you may get spotted and end up as someone else's lunch!

Keeping up our feline façade is only possible because we find ways to dissociate ourselves from our harmful actions. We trick ourselves into thinking that decisions – like sacking people in the interests of efficiency, refusing a charity request or killing off a piece of Nature – are not personal. We hire impersonal management consultants to do the dirty work for us. We rationalise that we are pawns on the chequerboard of the economy, the international markets, the shareholders, the budget, the performance appraisal form, or the corporate bonus system. Hence, while dishing out pain to others, we go on to accept a healthy salary increase and additional perks. Then we feed ourselves on another course of equally self-serving illusions – like managers are more valuable than the workers; like only those who create the wealth should share in the spoils; like there have to be winners and losers; and if there were no material incentives, who would work?

Elephant companies do not allow their people to hide behind convenient corporate masks. They do not profess values that they do not believe in or practise. Instead, they make it uncomfortable to think or act like a lion. Not by writing warm fuzzy value statements, or by throwing the rulebook at transgressors. Instead, they use two old-fashioned, tried and tested techniques – leading by example and applying collective moral pressure.

Take America's popular ice-cream chain, Ben & Jerry's Homemade Inc, for example. Since equity in the workplace was one of their fundamental values, the founders insisted on a top to bottom salary ratio of 7:1. Although the arrival of a new CEO in 1995 pushed up the ratio to 14:1, this was still commendably egalitarian compared with the rest of corporate America where CEOs were earning on average 85 times more than their employees. Staff diversity was another value, but not just on paper. By the mid-1990s, the number of minorities employed at Ben & Jerry's was three per cent, almost double the 1.8 per cent that made up the Vermont population. Three per cent of professionals and managers were also from minority groups, including the CEO. The percentage of women in senior and professional positions was 40 per cent and the company paid these women 37.5 per cent more than the national average.

Giving is another instance in which Ben & Jerry's put their money where their values are. In one year they committed as much as 7.5 per cent of pre-tax profits in donations to charity, compared with around one per cent for the US food and manufacturing sector as a whole. Seeking to live up to their social responsibility values, Ben & Jerry's have also invited a succession of social responsibility experts over the years to publish an independent commentary on the company's social performance.

Another great example of elephant values in action is Brazil's largest marine and food-processing machinery manufacturer, Semco. Under the innovative leadership of company president Ricardo Semler, Semco lives and breathes three fundamental values – democracy, shared prosperity and transparency. These values are based on the notion of giving employees control over their own lives. "We hire adults," says Semler in his autobiography *Maverick*, "and then we treat them like adults." Putting these values into practice has resulted in some serious corporate shapeshifting. For starters, the councillors (equivalent to what lion companies call executive directors) take it in six-month turns to act as CEO in cycles that overlap, rather than coincide with budgetary cycles. Associates (lower level employees) often earn more than coordinators (managers) or partners (divisional heads) and can increase their recognition and rewards without having to be part of line management.

All Semco employees attend classes to learn how to read and understand 'the numbers' and each and every one receives the accounts for their division each month. Staff are also given access on request to any other company information, including everyone else's salaries. "If people are embarrassed by their salaries," reasons Semler, "that probably means they aren't earning them." Semco has a similar open-house attitude to information leakage into the market. "After all, why worry about yesterday's news?" Semco has done away with hourly pay and now everyone gets a monthly salary, which they are allowed to participate in setting themselves. Semco distributes a half-yearly salary market survey and says: "Figure out where you stand on this thing. You know what you do; you know what everyone else in the company makes; you know what you need; you know what's fair. Come back on Monday and tell us what to pay you." Those that belong to unions have their salaries negotiated collectively. Furthermore, each division in Semco has a separate profit-sharing programme. Twice a year, they put aside 23 per cent of the after-tax profit of each division and decide – by simple majority vote – what to do with it. In most units the decision has ended up being one of equal distribution among all the workers in the division. Hence, the person who sweeps the floor gets as much as the division's partner.

Of course, corporate values seldom exist in isolation from broader cultural values. It is hardly surprising that modern capitalist enterprises display the values of Leo when the Western culture that produced them embodies such a conquering ethic. For this very reason, non-Western cultures may be on the brink of a renaissance as their more elephant-oriented values become increasingly valuable. This contrast is nowhere more pronounced than between the so-called Western/Northern countries and those of the South/East. For example, the culture of the West/North is highly focused on individual performance and rewards hierarchical authority and rational decision-making, while the East/South's emphasis is more about social harmony and cohesion, participative decision-making, creative expression and motivation.

The American Dream of rags to riches through individual hard work and personal achievement is but one symbol of the West/North's lion values. In business, most of us operate under these values every day, so they will not be explored further. But consider the alternatives. In Japanese culture, there is the concept of *wa* which stresses group harmony and social cohesion and *ringi* (meaning root-binding) which describes a bottom-up approach to decision-making. This outlook on life translates into business practices that value consensus and unity of purpose, service and loyalty to a larger whole (the company, the country, the world), and cooperation between individuals and groups in the workplace. An objection may be made here that we praised Japan to the skies for these values in the 1970s and 1980s as they conquered the world's markets with their zero-defect cars, TVs, VCRs and Walkmans. Then the wheels came off in the 1990s and they're still off. But one shouldn't confuse the good characteristics we are talking about with the deficiencies that have caused the Japanese economy to crash – an inflexible attitude towards structural changes and an emphasis on copycatting Western technology rather than doing original research and development.

In Africa, there is the widespread value of *ubuntu*, which is based on a proverb meaning 'a person becomes human through other people'. Zimbabwean business leader and author, Lovemore Mbigi, speaks of "emancipating the spirit of *ubuntu* by building a culture based on tolerance, respect, human dignity and solidarity". Similarly, South African executive, Reuel Khoza, describes *ubuntu* as the philosophy of "I am because you are; you are because we are." It is a concept, he says, "which brings to the fore images of supportiveness, cooperation, and solidarity, that is, communalism".

According to Mbigi, *ubuntu* is supported by a host of related sociocultural ideas from the African heritage such as *illima* (a cooperative effort in plowing), *inquina* (hunting as a team), and *ukudla* (sharing food). Similarly, there is the practice of *ukisisa* or 'cows never die'. According to this principle, when a poor person in the community is encountered, the dignity of that person is protected by someone who is better endowed with cattle-wealth communicating the need for one of his or her cows to be cared for. This transaction in turn provides the destitute member with milk and wealth in the form of one or two calves, after which the original cow is 'borrowed back'. The practical application of such elephant-friendly values in business is a golden thread that runs through the remainder of this chapter.

6.2 *Vision: A jumbo quest*

Shapeshifting seldom happens in countries or companies without visionary leadership. Like the revolutionary philosophers and scientists of centuries past, somebody has to be able to step outside of the parochial present and see the bigger picture of the future. And like those historical reformers, today's innovative leaders walk a tightrope between being recognised and celebrated as visionaries and being regarded as crackpots to be locked up or heathens to be burned at the stake.

The great thing about creating a sustainable future is that it is an inspiring ideal: something that, like the elephant, is bigger than ourselves – a little frightening, somehow magical, an exciting challenge at the very least. And in today's barren desert of materialism and secularism, people are crying out for something inspirational, even sacred, to quench their thirst for meaning. Sustainability is that oasis shimmering on the horizon. It is what we call the 'wow calling', the hunger for something to believe in, the eternal yearning to make a positive difference.

Often, this profound revelation is accomplished through partaking in a 'vision quest'. The vision quest is a sacred ritual common to many ancient indigenous cultures. It is performed at critical times in the life of an individual, such as entering adulthood, choosing a vocation or becoming an elder. Likewise, the vision quest can apply at a community level, when a tribe are seeking peace, needing rain or changing their leadership ranks. The traditional process goes something like this. The questers leave the safe environment of their community and travel to a remote, isolated place. Alone in this wilderness environment, as they fast and pit themselves against the elements, they begin to face their psychological fears and emotional demons. These invisible trials prepare their consciousness to receive a vision. The revelation may come as a sign, a symbol, a dream or a vision. It may manifest as a cloud shape or an animal messenger or simply a 'thought-quake'. When the questers return, the diviner and the elders help to interpret their visions and reveal what new meaning it heralds for the life of the individual or the community.

With the era of sustainability looming as a new stage in the life of business and nations, companies and countries need to go on their own vision quest. This could take many different forms: a personal Damascus-type experience by the CEO or president, perhaps catalysed by his or her children or grandchildren; demands for a policy response to a major strategic change such as clearer evidence that carbon consumption should be constrained; or a paradigm shift in the wake of a crisis such as the terrorist attack on New York on September 11, 2001.

Interface, a Fortune 1000 company and the world's largest producer of contract commercial carpets, is a good example of the potency of discovering an inspiring vision. In 1973, Ray Anderson left an executive position with a well-known US carpet manufacturer and risked his life savings and the investments of good friends to found his own company, which became Interface. By 1994, the company was already extremely successful but it began to hear a strange rumble in the wind – inquiries from customers about the environmental aspects of Interface's products. Interface, like many companies have done, stood on the cusp of a strategic decision. They could ignore the rumbling, believing it to be a bit of harmless corporate indigestion (which is to be expected with a growing appetite for profits). Or they could listen more carefully. After all, it might be an approaching tidal wave! Then again, it could also be a form of intelligent communication like the infrasonic language of elephants on the horizon. Needless to say, Anderson heard the call – if somewhat reluctantly at first.

The company's research arm had been charged with coming up with an environmental policy. They in turn asked Anderson, as CEO at the time, to launch the environmental task force by giving them an environmental vision. Anderson recalls that he didn't want to make that speech because he had no vision other than compliance with the law. Then he came across Paul Hawken's book, *The Ecology of Commerce*, and felt its message he recalls "like a spear in the chest". Anderson claims that "in a heartbeat" he had found the vision he was looking for, together with a powerful sense of urgency to implement it. He saw that business was part of the problem and part of the solution. And he had the courage to say: "Someone has to take the lead! Why not us?" Anderson offered the task force a vision: to make Interface the first name in industrial ecology worldwide through substance, not words. And he gave them a mission too: to convert Interface into a 'restorative enterprise'. First, Interface would attain a state of sustainability, and then it would become restorative by putting back more than the company takes from the Earth by helping others to reach sustainability – even competitors. How he translated this vision into practice is dealt with in a later section of this chapter.

The provocative vision of Anita Roddick, founder of the international cosmetics company, The Body Shop, is another example of how shapeshifting can be catalysed. "As far as I am concerned," she says in her book *Business as Unusual*, "the business has existed for one reason only – to allow us to use our success to act as a force for social change, to contribute to the education and consciousness-raising of our staff, to assist development in the Third World and, above all, to help protect the environment. What we are trying to do is to create a new business paradigm, simply showing that business can have a human face and a social conscience."

She goes on to say that for The Body Shop the business of business is to keep the company alive and breathlessly excited; to protect the workforce; to be a force for good in society and then think about the speculators. She believes that if companies are in business solely to make money, you can't fully trust whatever else they do or say. She sees business as a renaissance concept, where the human spirit comes into play. It does not have to be drudgery; it does not have to be the science of making money. It can be something that people genuinely feel good about, but only if it remains a human enterprise.

"How do you ennoble the spirit when you are selling something as inconsequential as a cosmetic cream?" asks Roddick rhetorically. She answers that you do it by creating a sense of holism or spiritual development, of feeling connected to the workplace and the environment and of forging relationships with one another. It's how to make Monday to Friday a sense of being alive rather than a slow death. How do you give people a chance to do a good job? By making them feel good about what they are doing. The spirit soars when you are satisfying your own basic material needs in such a way that you are also serving the needs of others honourably and humanely. And she adds: "Under these circumstances, I can even feel great about a moisturizer." Of course, her detractors will argue that she has had to step down from pole position in the company precisely because she wasn't businesslike enough in conducting the company's affairs. They will point to the very disappointing performance of the share price over the last ten years. And they will gloat over the fact that her downfall was brought about by the supermarket chains that she derided. Yet, there is no denying that she has left an indelible mark on the corporate world and that she is not done with her shapeshifting career yet. While giving up her hands-on role, she is staying on as a nonexecutive director and consultant at the Body Shop and will no doubt continue her campaign for principled leadership in business.

In South Africa, the Spier company is another example of visionary elephant leadership. Set in the idyllic landscape of Stellenbosch in the Cape, Spier had operated as a wine farm for three centuries before the (then) 90-hectare estate was bought by businessman Dick Enthoven. Having led an extremely successful career in South Africa's mainstream business sector, Enthoven wanted to leave a legacy, to give something back. Transforming Spier became the centrepoint of his vision quest. "In 150 years from now," says Enthoven, "I want people to look back and say that they did a good job."

The way this vision has unfolded in practice is a colourful story full of inspiration. It started with Enthoven embracing the cultural heritage of the area. Spier set about restoring the old Cape-Dutch historical buildings on the estate that date back to 1680, and turning these into conference and restaurant facilities. Next, a hotel complex named The Village was constructed, drawing on the Cape's Malay influences for its architectural style and on ecological principles for its design. An open-air amphitheatre was also built and an Arts Trust started to develop and showcase local talent. The last initiative led to the recent performance of *Carmen* in the West End of London by a South African cast of newcomers, which drew rave reviews from music critics of leading English newspapers.

One of Enthoven's key concerns in the Spier project was "the restoration of equity in a society that has been distorted by social engineering". For this reason, former farm labourers have been given an ownership and management stake in the vineyards and vegetable farming enterprises. In addition, Spier has embarked on establishing an off-site eco-village, which will eventually incorporate schools, offices, craft workshops, an arts venue, a community centre and homes for almost 150 local families.

There have been various ecological reforms at Spier as well. With 140 hectares of land set aside for organic farming, it is now one of the largest commercial organic farms in South Africa, cultivating both vegetables and vines. Spier has also formed a subsidiary called Green Technologies which acquired the South African licence for an environmentally-friendly waste treatment system called the Biolytix Filter. The installation of this Biolytic Filtration system at The Village at Spier is the first of its kind on this scale in the world.

The vision around which Enthoven has been building Spier's renaissance is now classic triple bottom line thinking, underpinned by a set of inspiring values. The latter include the following: custodians of culture; financial viability and economic sustainability; unexpected pleasures; places of the soul; sustainable resource use; community building; and learning for development. As 'airy fairy' as these values may sound, Eve Annecke, who is the Spier executive responsible for implementing them in all operations, can certainly not be accused of living with her head in the clouds. "We are not on some sort of moral trip here," she says. "We're dealing with practical technologies and looking for better ways of doing things. We learn as we go and we face contradictions all the time: what good is organic farming when women are subject to regular abuse at home, or when babies are born with foetal alcohol syndrome? We live in a violent society. We are not pretending to solve all the problems but we are acknowledging that the problems exist and we work at resolving them where we can."

Adrian Enthoven, chairman of Spier Holdings and a director of Biolytix, sums up their philosophy as follows: "Our view is not purely altruistic. The whole world is moving in this direction – towards ecological sustainability. Economic imperatives are driving it, and economics relies on social sustainability. These three issues are inextricably linked and this is why, at Spier, we call for accountability in terms of the triple bottom line: financial viability, social equity and ecological sustainability."

There are numerous other examples of companies that have experienced successful vision quests involving sustainability. Ryuzaburo Kaku, former chairman of the Canon group of companies, speaks for all of these pioneers when he muses that, in the highest stage of evolution of a corporation, "a global consciousness emerges and the corporation sees itself contributing to the whole of mankind". This is founded on the Japanese philosophy of *Kyosei* – living and working together for the common good. Jumbo visions such as these act like sprinklings of magic dust in the business of shapeshifting. They work not because they intellectually convince us, but because they emotionally engage us and spiritually inspire us. They work because we are all, as humans, on a vision quest for meaning in our lives.

6.3 *Work: An elephants' playground?*

Having a leader's inspiring vision is one thing, but it is like whistling in the wind unless people in the workplace are able to express their own inherent magic – their creativity and imagination, their values and passions. As Anita Roddick says: "People become motivated when you guide them to the source of their own power."

And yet lion companies don't seem all that interested in the personal magic of their employees. The problem is that magic is, well, a bit unpredictable (and a tad scary too). It cannot be reliably channelled in service of the almighty buck. And it usually involves a lot of flaky intuition and gooey emotions. I mean, how can hunting be efficient if it is subject to the whims of a muse or constantly distracted by feelings of compassion for the other animals? No, when employees are at work, they must be constantly reminded of their mission: that they are lions hunting down prey – customers, market share, profits, anything that glitters. They must focus on the corporate mission, the sales objectives, the quarterly review. Time is money. Therefore, they must be strongly discouraged from spending any work-time on socialising, resting, playing, eating, or attending to personal matters. They must do those things *after hours* (as if life after work doesn't really take place in *real* time).

The ideal employee of the lion company is one who arrives at work (early), checks in his or her personal life at the door, and goes straight into profit-making overdrive. It helps with the focus if the employees can switch off their feelings as well, since work is a place for rational individuals. And as for creativity and intuition, well, we talked about that already. It's not that they are bad as such. It's just that they are so difficult to control, and they don't translate easily into consultants' mantras, data tables and bar charts. If the truth be told, they're just not very macho.

There *is* a problem of course – humans! They are not machines or computers. In fact, they almost insist on being unfocused. And, as a general rule, they are not very rational either. They have emotions! Not to mention all their distracting demands – no work on weekends, big chunks of idle leave, irresponsible bouts of illness and pension payments when they become worn out. That's why lion companies have ingeniously invented a multitude of bribery mechanisms (incremental salary increases, incentive bonuses, pretentious job titles, offices with a door and even a view) and behavioural rules (policies, procedures, systems). In return, of course many employees of lion companies adopt their own version of lion-like behaviour. When they go to the office, they 'go to war' with all their rivals. Or they work to rule. Or they chisel extras out of their travel and expense accounts on the basis that if the company is going to be a predator, so can I.

Elephant companies, on the other hand, do something that is almost unimaginable. They accept humans as humans. They don't try to turn us into machines. In fact, they encourage us to express all aspects of our humanness. For example, they realise that we function according to natural rhythms, not artificial clock time – we all have cycles of productivity over the course of a day. We are also remarkably good at multiprocessing and multitasking: they stimulate us and keep us from getting tired, bored and unproductive.

In an elephant work environment, there is no fussing about start times and end times, or being in the office versus working at home. There is no need to feel guilty about attending to the odd 'distraction'. Employees don't build up stress as they do in lion companies because all the bits and pieces of life are being neglected – like family and household chores and personal banking. Don't get us wrong: elephant companies do not offer a licence for slackness and corruption. By treating their staff as responsible adults, the latter apply their own codes of conduct, which are probably stricter than the external rules would be, to themselves. They feel a sense of duty, they have self-discipline! Thus, it is often hard to tell 'work' apart from 'personal' or 'fun' or any other lifestyle choice in an elephant company, whereas lion companies prefer to put them in boxes.

Elephants' fuzziness is very frustrating to a lion manager of course. Elephants seem to just mosey around all day, nibbling a bit of this, dusting a bit of that, chatting to some friends here, splashing around in a mud hole there. They are not focused on the prey at all. Look at all that time they take for family bonding, for having fun in the water, for catching up with the gossip from passing friends. There's none of the stress of being a hunter. Mind you, they don't starve. In fact, they seem to do very well despite not being obsessed about food. Mmm, interesting! One CEO of an elephant company has Walt Disney mementoes all around his office, which he calls his playroom. In particular, he has a large effigy of Mickey Mouse next to his desk. This is to remind all the important people who come to see him that he is head of a Mickey Mouse company that wants to have some fun!

The aforementioned Semco allows its employees to control their own working conditions. Time clocks have been eliminated, and people come and go according to their own schedules – even on the factory floor. The result is greater spontaneous coordination between workers, and more people who can now do several jobs. Interestingly, although they set their own schedules and targets (or perhaps *because* they do), they tend to work longer hours to meet them. The success of this 'factory floor flexitime' is summed up by one of Semler's comments: "When we introduced flexible hours, we decided to hold regular follow-up meetings to track problems and decide how to deal with abuses and production interruptions. That was years ago, and we haven't yet held that first meeting."

So, working like an elephant is *not* about becoming completely scattered and ineffective. It *is* about being flexible, discovering the most appropriate times to work and play and socialise, or to do a combination of these. When we reconnect with our natural rhythms and apply them to our work, we play to our own individual strengths. At the same time, we work out ways to find a harmonious blend with each other's natural cycles. This increases, not decreases, our productivity. The reason is that we are not spending vast amounts of energy fighting our own natural tendencies. At the moment, most of us in lion workplaces feel obliged to persevere with rolling rocks up a hill in the morning, even though we know that in the afternoon the landscape will be flatter and the rocks will feel lighter. Shapeshifting will mean sloughing off some of the lion's control-freak habits, trusting others more, and having a less regimented environment.

Being human at work is also about being able to *be* ourselves – our whole selves. Lion companies take their cue from neoclassical economics and assume that people are 'free, rational utility-maximising individuals'. "Professionalism in management is regularly equated with hard-headed rationality", noted the Tom Peters and Robert Waterman duo of *In Search of Excellence* fame. "The problem with the rationalist view of organising people," they went on to say, "is that people are not very rational." To fit Frederick Taylor's old model of scientific management or today's organisational charts, they concluded that a human is simply designed wrong or, of course, vice versa, according to how you argue it. "In fact, if our understanding of the current state of psychology is even close to correct, man is the ultimate study in conflict and paradox."

The successful performance of split-brain surgery in the 1960s and 1970s seems to confirm this view, as well as to lend further insight. In treating 25 patients for severe epilepsy, doctors found that not only can the two hemispheres of our brain operate independently, but they also seem to control essentially opposite functions. While the left brain is associated with rational and intellectual engagements, the right brain is oriented towards intuitive and creative processes. Canadian business professor, Henry Mintzberg, was the first to spot the implications for business which he set forth in a 1976 article in the *Harvard Business Review* called 'Planning on the Left Side and Managing on the Right'. "The key managerial processes," he remarks, "are enormously complex and mysterious, drawing on the vaguest of information and using the least articulated mental processes. These processes seem more relational and holistic than ordered and sequential, and more intuitive than intellectual; they seem to be most characteristic of right-hemispheric activity."

This theme of duality and balance is one that the ancient Chinese understood well and is represented in their Tai Chi symbol, which depicts the flow of opposites within a greater whole. Contained within the circular symbol, the one extreme, *yang*, represents masculine, active, competitive and rigid characteristics; while *yin* encapsulates the feminine, passive, cooperative and flexible aspects. Lions are *yang*; elephants are *yin*. And most of today's companies are *yang* companies, praising 'hard' qualities like rationality and assertiveness, and pooh-poohing 'soft' traits like intuition and compassion.

It is not difficult to diagnose whether your company is a lion or an elephant. Just count the number of times words like 'love' and 'caring' and 'morality' crop up in management meetings; or how often people feel comfortable enough to cry at the office. Former head of chemical giant ICI once said that the word 'love' was as threatening in business as talking about an unexpected liability on the balance sheet. Author and Fortune 500 company director, James Autry, makes the same point in his inspiring book, *Love & Profit*. Feelings are seen as a weakness in the testosterone-dominated corporate world. One chairman was reported to have asked a colleague why one of his managers had left the business to join the church. His colleague replied: "Long-term promotion prospects." It hadn't occurred to the chairman that there might be life after the company!

For lions, displaying toughness is all-important. And toughness means dominating meetings and markets, intimidating suppliers and competitors, controlling situations and people. Toughness means showing intellectual superiority and aggressive ambition and not letting emotions cloud your judgement. Elephants, on the other hand, are led by matriarchs. Emotions are openly displayed within the herd – be they affection, grief or delight. Extrasensory perception is constantly relied upon. Nurturing intimate relationships is all-important.

Trying to turn complex, variable humans into rational, predictable machines has left many people feeling like prisoners, trapped in their jobs, unable to be who they really are. Certainly, given the choice, it is not how they would choose to spend their lives. But there's the mortgage to think about, the school fees, the parents' expectations. Even beyond that, so many people we talk to experience feelings of existential crisis in their work. "What it's all about, Alfie?" they plaintively ask, just as songstress Cilla Black did in the 1960s. Incidentally, she was picked out from the crowd by Brian Epstein, the same man who discovered The Beatles in the Cavern in Liverpool. Just an elephant aside!

One thing that would help with the existential crisis in business would be a switch from the present focus on 'jobs' to the old idea of 'vocations'. A job is something you do to earn money to get by. It is a means to an end. Thus, people often end up 'living for the weekend' or counting down the days to their retirement. A vocation, on the other hand, is a life pursuit that you do out of a sense of calling, a feeling of being uniquely suited for performing a certain kind of work. Mythologist Joseph Campbell talked about "following your bliss". How many people can use that word to describe their work – bliss! You may think that we are spiralling off into a dream world here, an idealist's fantasy. But stay with us. Pursuing a vocation should not be mistaken for some kind of hallucinatory happiness trip, free of all cares, worries, stresses or difficulties. In many ways, following your bliss is more difficult, because it entails soul-searching, tenacious endurance, constant questioning, facing fears, shrugging off securities and stretching every fibre of your being. The difference is that it feels like a personal quest, a freely chosen path, a journey with a purpose. Intuitively, we are all searching for this Holy Grail in our careers, hobbies or voluntary work.

The experiences of Victor Frankl, outlined in his book *Man's Search for Meaning*, provide some insight into this heartfelt yearning of ours to make something meaningful of our work. Frankl, a trained psychiatrist, lived through the Nazi concentration camps, and noticed that people can endure the most trying and horrific circumstances if they can discover and nurture a sense of personal meaning. Providing, therefore, there is something to believe in, the human spirit triumphs over physical hardship or emotional trauma. The 'something' can be anything – the achievement of a personal goal, the development of a particular skill, the creation of something unique or beautiful, or the pursuit of a spiritual quest. But the essential feature is that it is a personal belief. No one can tell you what should inspire you or motivate you. No one can brainwash you into discovering meaning in your work if it's not your bag. No one can pre-select your vocation for you. Of course, the lion economy makes the pursuit of vocations very difficult. Round people are put in square holes because nobody consulted them about their true desires. Hence, once again, the need for multilevel shapeshifting.

6.4 *Governance: Council of the animals*

Governance is a word that lions don't like much. It smacks too much of giving away power. Or sharing supper. Lion directors prefer the freedom of making all their decisions in secret councils or while they're on the run, with no justification needed and no recourse back to them. Why should they consult beyond their colleagues in the inner sanctum on whether to swallow up another company, or shut down an operation and retrench thousands of workers? These are strategic matters that only the board can decide on. The pride rules.

Lions want power and autonomy, not for their own sake they are quick to add; but because they need to make things *happen* and fast. Opportunities and threats come and go at cheetah-like speed, whether they are stock market fluctuations, competitor tactics, product innovations or customer fashions. Markets are like the gun-toting Wild West. Fastest on the draw stays alive and lives to chew another roll of tobacco. Not to mention pocketing a bit of the 'ole booty' along the way. Doing business is a verb, not an adjective: it is active not passive. Feline companies pounce in the twitch of a whisker.

In other words, if the lion king has his way, business is a monarchy, not a democracy. He rules by divine right, issuing edicts from his royal court of directors. And what good is it being a powerful lion king if you have to explain your every action to the masses? Or account for the origin and size of your obvious opulence? Lion kings exist to rule *over* their subjects; to direct their destiny and control their lives – their daily tasks, their dress code, their beliefs and their lifestyle. The people must be made to serve with unquestioning loyalty and contribute towards the overheads of running the royal court. And if they disobey, the long arm of the 'paw' will catch up with them.

To question a lion's choice of prey or hunting style is to invite getting your head bitten off. Lions expect everyone to trust their feline instincts and appetite-driven judgements unreservedly. After all, no lion ever caught an antelope (or conquered a country, or captured a market) by asking the buffalo for advice, or sitting around a thorn tree discussing it with the warthog, or asking permission from the rhinoceros. And those who would criticise the laws of the jungle should reserve their irritating chatter for the monkeys; maybe *they* will listen. This starts to get down to the heart of the governance debate, namely the dual issues of control and transparency. You don't need to ask a lion who should be in charge! But if you are a springbok or a zebra or a giraffe, you may want to have a say in the way that the bushveld is run. In particular, you may want to question the lion's right to kill off whomsoever he pleases, whensoever he pleases. Or his right to fatten himself and his pride, while the rest of the animals are starving during a drought. Or to be the growling censor of any information put out by the company on how it is run. Extracting facts is like extracting teeth – difficult when it's the lion's mouth you're trying to get them out of!

However, the seeds of a popular revolt have been planted with the anti-globalisation demonstrations in Seattle in 1999 serving as a sign of things to come. And the demonstrations have got worse despite a growing security shield around each 'high and mighty' meeting. The frustration and anger about the unhealthy power balance in the world has boiled over (with increasing violence) in every city where the Political Establishment have met. Quite simply, the gap is getting too wide between the rich and the poor countries and between the rich and the poor within countries. For their part, the corporate lions participate annually in noble-sounding debates at the World Economic Forum, licking their paws and knowing full well that they will never be called upon to implement any resolutions that come out of it. They will be free to go on as they please.

Companies have become more powerful than governments. Yet, the millions whose lives they affect have little or no say in what they do. The public do not choose which companies are allowed to exist and operate in their communities, nor do they elect the directors and managers. Yes, they do buy the company's products and services as consumers and are free to switch from one company to another. But, as we've emphasised already, the 'invisible hand' of the market exerts limited pressure. The only real accountability that business has is to itself and its lion-leaning shareholders. If, as a result of corporate actions, national economies go into crisis, or communities suffer, or the environment is degraded, it is seldom that the shareholders and company directors go into battle against one another. The share price has to drop for that to happen. The shenanigans at Enron would never have become public if Enron had not gone bust as a result.

But the world is shapeshifting to some extent. Elephant activists are trumpeting their concerns loudly enough for the lions finally to be taking notice. Over the past decade, for example, numerous corporate governance codes have emerged which require companies to give a more transparent account of how their business is being run and the impacts on the various stakeholder groups. One of the most recent and progressive documents is South Africa's revised King Report, which even makes explicit recommendations on sustainability reporting and social and ethical accountability. Shapeshifting goes beyond putting ticks into boxes, however. At the end of the day, it is once again about values and behaviour. Companies that perpetuate the widening gap between rich and poor in their own payroll profile are always going to fall into the lions' camp. Companies that persist in managing from the top down will never turn their fangs into tusks. And companies that only create partnerships that benefit themselves may learn to purr, but they will never lose their roar. Elephant companies, on the other hand, embrace the principles and practices of good governance with passion. They worry less about controlling and more about caring and sharing. They volunteer; they don't grudgingly concede.

In order to implement governance at a practical level, shapeshifting needs to occur in at least three areas: company incentive systems, decision-making processes and communication methods. In exploring these issues, it is instructive once again to contrast Western and Southern cultural dynamics. For example, in traditional African culture, it is socially undesirable and inappropriate to behave so as to 'stand out from the crowd' in the way that individual achievement is promoted in Anglo-Saxon culture. The reason is that such behaviour may destroy vital social cohesion in a community by creating destructive competition or undermining the respected role of the elders in the tribe.

This is not to say that individuals are not encouraged to master areas in which they display a particular aptitude or natural gift. On the contrary, skilful specialisation, whether as a healer, artist, hunter or leader, has always been a key element in enabling communities to survive and thrive. But the context for this achievement is carefully managed, through strict social rules, in order to ensure that it enhances the common good and maintains the cohesion of the unit. Contrast this with the stereotypical reward system in the West that tends to be based on individual merit regardless of what it does to the rest of the team.

Cashbuild is a pioneering South African company that showed how elephant thinking could be put into practice in business long before corporate governance had become a catch phrase. For instance, in the 1980s they revised their performance appraisal system so that they were "geared to rewarding team achievements whilst also rewarding individual contributions to the improvement of the functioning of the team as a whole. In this way, the poor and mediocre performers are encouraged to raise their standards, in contrast to the situation where higher performers lower their standards to maintain their identification with the group."

According to former managing director of Cashbuild, Albert Koopman, replacing reward and punishment systems with systems based on peer recognition and rejection makes good business sense. For example, under Cashbuild's old reward/punishment system, the company could never reduce employee absenteeism and lost hours to a figure below 15 per cent despite repeated warning letters and disciplinary procedures. Then, when they used the peer group concept by simply placing red marks next to late or absent employees' names on a publicly displayed chart (with no management reprimand), lost hours immediately dropped to one per cent.

Cashbuild also introduced other innovative practices. They held extensive 'sharing' sessions among employees, aimed at deepening understanding of diverse histories, cultures and values in the workplace. They removed the power imbalance in management-labour relations through the empowerment of shop steward committees and other representative councils. And once a year, the company held a three-day communal gathering, 'The Great Indaba', during which every employee had the opportunity to make his or her views on Cashbuild and its leadership heard. This sharing approach resulted in consensus being reached more quickly on key decisions. In the one year, it took a mere 35 minutes to conclude wage negotiations.

The Brazilian company Semco, to which reference was made earlier in this chapter, also shows how to take democracy seriously in the workplace. The company does not hire or promote people until they have been interviewed and accepted by all their future subordinates. Twice a year, subordinates evaluate their immediate managers and everyone in the company fills out an anonymous questionnaire about corporate credibility and top management competence. In addition, all important decisions are made collegially – sometimes even by a company-wide vote.

Of course, given the latest advances in computer networks which allow for real-time feedback, it is considerably easier to implement workplace democracy. But the battle-scarred lions have to let go of their control first. The great elephant leader and former South African president, Nelson Mandela, gives some clues to this new governance style in his autobiographical *Long Walk to Freedom*. He recounts his childhood memories of how tribal meetings allowed for full participation by every Thembu person of the region, without interruption or intervention by the regent chief. He reflects on how these early experiences have influenced his own approach to governance as follows: "As a leader, I have always followed the principles I saw demonstrated by the regent at the Great Place. I have always endeavoured to listen to what each and every person in a discussion had to say before venturing my own opinion. Oftentimes, my own opinion will simply represent a consensus of what I heard in the discussion." Mandela always remembered the regent's axiom: a leader is like a shepherd. He stays behind the flock, letting the most nimble go on ahead, whereupon the others follow, not realising that all along they are being directed from behind.

6.5 *Relationships: Walking gently as giants*

Elephants are highly sociable creatures. They move in large herds, which usually comprise more than one family group. They protect, care for and even suckle each other's young. In the dry season, several herds will often join together or remain in infrasonic contact. It's almost as if they believe that camaraderie helps them face the harsh elements of Nature. A lot of their time and energy is spent cultivating and nurturing relationships in the herd, whether by frequent infrasonic dialogue, playing together or intimate caresses with their trunks. It is clear that building bonds of family and friendship is at least as important as feeding. In the wider context, they have no natural enemies and many of their actions are symbiotic in nature, such as digging water holes, fertilising ingested seeds and making vegetation accessible to other species.

In terms of our metaphor, lions also have relationships, although they tend to see their opposite numbers more like self-serving acquaintances. Team building in the pride is important for effective pack hunting. Cubs will be looked after, so long as they are effective predators. But friendship doesn't extend much beyond the family. After all, other prides are competitors chasing after the same food. And other species are either competitors or prey, or accomplices. When mixing does occur, it is usually brief and unemotional with survival in mind. For the lion, procreation is hardly a romantic affair – wham, bam and not even 'thank you, ma'am'. And as for relationships with other creatures, well, who can trust a lion? No matter how smoothly he purrs, there is always the chance of your being 'friend today, food tomorrow'.

In business, the dynamics have been the same. Companies have cultivated relationships only from pure self-interest – mostly with shareholders, financial analysts, customers and suppliers. And usually, these interactions have been a pure power play – wining and dining the influential few, while ignoring the rest or pressuring them into conformance. The idea of genuine dialogue with communities, NGOs and government for the sake of enduring symbiotic relationships, rather than as a short-term bargaining tactic, is still somewhat unpalatable for most companies. With their quarterly eye on the skittish profits, spending time and energy on building long-term friendships without any immediate reward seems, well, a costly indulgence.

But the game is changing. To survive in the sustainability era, companies have to move beyond their aggressive, competitive tendencies. They need to learn to be not only sociable, but genuinely concerned about the perspectives and wellbeing of *all* of their stakeholders. Barry Nalebuff and Adam Brandenburger, in their book of the same title, call this transition *Co-opetition*, while David Wheeler and Maria Sillanpää talk about *The Stakeholder Corporation* and Paul

Hawken, Amory B. Lovins and L. Hunter Lovins about *Natural Capitalism*.

Companies ignore this friendly advice at their own peril. Stakeholders, if maltreated, can bite back, and even the most macho multinational lions can find themselves bleeding. Already, the casualty list of high-profile companies is long – BP, Dreamworks, Green Cross, Intel, McDonald's, Monsanto, Nike, Proctor & Gamble, Shell, Texaco and Wal-Mart, to mention but a few. Encouragingly, however, the list of 'branded' stakeholder-oriented shapeshifters is also growing, including the likes of 3M, AT&T, The Body Shop, Canon, Electrolux, Hewlett Packard, Levi Strauss, Reebok, Unilever, Volkswagen and Volvo.

Employees are such core stakeholders to business that transgressions on this front are almost unforgivable. Texaco found this out when a racism scandal in 1996 lost its shareholders more than $1 billion in market capitalisation on the day the news broke and ultimately cost the company $115 million in a legal settlement of a suit filed on behalf of 1 400 employees. Likewise, Wal-Mart and Nike sustained heavy damage to their reputations when their contractors were caught employing cheap child labour in Third World countries. It didn't help Nike's public relations nightmare that it paid sports celebrity Michael Jordan $20 million a year to endorse their products, while paying its Indonesian contract labour annual wages of less than $1 000.

A similar tale of employee neglect can be told about the asbestos mining industry. Companies like Turner & Newall (T&N) and Cape plc argued for years that the health risks to their workers were acceptable. The courts, however, are starting to side with former employees who are the victims of the occupational disease of asbestosis. T&N has already paid out more than £350 million over ten years to meet the claims of its former employees, and Cape plc recently reached a settlement agreement of £22 million to compensate the families of a group of former South African miners. One has to wonder whether other mining companies, as well as nuclear energy utilities and chemical companies, may suffer a similar fate in the elephant landscape of the future?

In contrast, Reebok, who has developed a reputation for taking a public stand on social issues, pledged to fight exploitative labour practices. It called on activists to alert it to any abuses that were occurring and began requesting all its vendors for certification that they were complying with codes of conduct, such as those of the International Labour Organisation. Levi Strauss has gone even further. In Bangladesh and Turkey, where children were working for contractors and providing their family's only source of income, Levi's actually paid the contractors to keep the children in school until they were fourteen. In areas where it felt it had less influence, like China, Levi's took the tough commercial decision to withdraw from the country until its human rights record improves.

In recognition of the importance of its employees, American telecommunications giant AT&T has introduced alternative measures of performance that include 'people value added', alongside 'customer value added' and 'economic value added'. Likewise, Swedish insurance company Skandia has begun to quantify its hidden assets by producing reports that place a financial value on its 'intellectual capital'. Meanwhile, Volkswagen is trying to balance the reliance on 'shareholder value' with the concept of 'workholder value'.

Customers are another major stakeholder group, which all companies swear they look after. But the evidence does not always agree. Take tobacco companies for instance, who at one point swore before Congress that they believed that cigarettes were not addictive. They are not so bold since the landmark court case in which Grady Carter was awarded $750 000 in damages for the loss of a lung following cancer surgery. This was one of the first in a string of liability claims against tobacco companies in 1996, resulting in losses in share value of billions of dollars (the value of British American Tobacco suddenly dropped by £3 billion alone).

Banks also have a notoriously bad track record with customers by failing to provide financial services to those who need them the most – the poor and socially marginalised population. Yet banks like the Los Angeles Community Development Bank, the South Shore Bank of Chicago, the Caja Labora in Spain, and the Grameen Bank in Bangladesh have shown that financial services can be made accessible to *all* customers, not just the lucrative 'high net worth' sector. Others, like the Cooperative Bank in the UK, VanCity in Vancouver, Citizens Bank in Tokyo and the Triodos Bank in Europe also show that customers' money can be made to 'work' for various sustainability causes, such as investing in community development and promoting renewable energy.

Suppliers are another key stakeholder group, and proactive engagement with the supply chain is going to become critical for elephant companies of the future. Early adopters of this new reality were The Body Shop, the Cooperative Bank, Traidcraft and Ben & Jerry's. More recently, companies like Unilever, Sainsbury's, Volvo and Nortel have joined the party. Unilever, which sells several ranges of fish products, has adopted a WWF-developed international labelling scheme for sustainable fish production, whereby its suppliers all need to be certified by the Marine Stewardship Council. This is a sister organisation to the highly successful certification scheme of the Forest Stewardship Council.

UK retailer Sainsbury's is also starting to scrutinise supplier relationships, insisting on 'dolphin friendly' tuna, organic vegetables and no animal testing. In the car-manufacturing sector, Volvo has added environmental care as the third of its core values that suppliers need to embrace, the other two being safety and quality. Telecommunications company Nortel emphasises partnerships with its suppliers in tackling the environmental impacts of its production chain. This 'shared savings' approach is being used to achieve a reduction in the use of chemicals in Canada and minimisation of waste in the UK.

The European Business Network for Social Cohesion is dedicated to walking as gently as giants. The network, comprising a coalition of more than 300 businesses including household names like British Telecom, Philips and Kellogg's, was established in 1995 to counteract the negative impacts of the global economy. They are a forum devoting their time to finding creative solutions that will help to avert redundancies, encourage employee reskilling, facilitate the reintroduction of laid-off employees into the workforce, and protect vulnerable economic groups. The UK's Business in the Community is a similar initiative.

Research by Harvard professors John Kotter and James Heskett confirms that taking care of stakeholders is good for the traditional bottom line as well. They compared the eleven-year records of large, established companies that gave customers, employees and shareholders equal priorities with those that always put their shareholders first. It turned out that the more stakeholder-sensitive companies grew sales four times faster, created eight times as many jobs, improved the share price eightfold and experienced greater net income growth. In other words, shapeshifting from a lion into an elephant is not the same as being condemned to starvation. Elephants have a healthy appetite;

they just aren't obsessed with food to the exclusion of everything and everyone else.

6.6 *Communication: The rumble in the jungle*

Lions don't communicate much except to roar to intimidate others or to purr with self-satisfaction. Likewise, modern companies have grown accustomed to speaking to stake-holders only on a 'need to know' basis – telling whom they want, what they want, when they want. Usually, this self-serving conversation coincides with a time when the company needs something from its stakeholders, such as support to proceed with a new development (or the absence of visible protest against it).

Elephant communication is quite different. It is more like dialogue: an ongoing, two-way, interactive process which involves listening as much as talking, and includes nonverbal as well as verbal exchange. Elephant companies are far less opportunistic when it comes to communicating with stakeholders. The reason they enter into dialogue with their employees, or communities, or environmental NGOs, is the fact that these entities are interconnected in some way, be they interested in, concerned about, or affected by the company's operations.

Elephant companies believe that the time when something goes wrong, or when they are required to consult – as in an accident, or spill, or downsizing, or a new project – is precisely the wrong time to *begin* communicating with stakeholders. By then, it is way too late. A symbiotic relationship already needs to be in place, one that has been nurtured over many years. To enable this 'getting to know you and trust you' process to bloom, there need to be all kinds of forums and feedback mechanisms that keep companies' finger on the pulse of stakeholders' issues and concerns. Attitude is also critical. Even having all the right communication tools may not be enough if these are only used to further preconceived company interests. Lions see stakeholders – whether labour unions or green activists – as whinging antelopes trying to curtail their appetite or cramp their hunting style. Hence, the feline communication strategy is usually to roar louder than the stakeholders and frighten them away or drown out the sound of their complaints. Failing this, other popular tactics are to ignore the stakeholders, discredit them, or hire a legal lion to hunt them down and eat them in the courts.

The elephant company's modus operandi is quite different, mainly because they believe that stakeholders actually have something valuable to say. In fact, the fresh perspective that the latter may bring could turn out to be a gift-wrapped opportunity. If they are saying that it is unacceptable to injure workers, or choke communities with pollution, or sell products that clog up the rivers, maybe that means that there is a market for safer, cleaner companies? After all, *all* stakeholders are customers too. Yet, it is not that stakeholders are always right and companies are always wrong. It's that companies and stakeholders are inextricably interconnected. Their destinies are so meshed together that there is no 'them' and 'us'. We are all one living system. And so long as we are all being honest and transparent about our objectives and opinions, working out the solutions to any dilemma – like the classic 'jobs versus environment' debate – becomes a cooperative effort among all stakeholders.

How different the actual world is! Often in the corporate sector's dealings with stakeholders, you feel you're in a crèche with babies babbling past each other or crying with frustration when nobody understands what they are trying to say. At one end of the table companies bawl out phrases like 'economic value added', 'gross margin on sales' and 'real return on capital employed', while at the other activist

NGOs return the fusillade with terms like 'social justice', 'intergenerational equity' and 'ecological sustainability'. In the end, each baby is left stomping its feet or wailing its heart out.

Any adult will understand that the missing ingredient is a common language that begins to construct a common outlook. Concepts like the triple bottom line, internalising externalities, stakeholder accountability, corporate governance and sustainable development are early attempts to develop a vocabulary that everyone can understand. But they still sound like jargon that will all too soon become unfashionable and forgotten. That is why we suggest a healthy dose of getting back to basics. Let's start by calling things what they are. Companies either 'care' about their stakeholders or they simply 'use' them for their own selfish gain.

Infants soon learn the important concepts in life – sharing and being selfish, playing and fighting, hurting and helping, being nice and being spiteful, laughing and crying. And what we try to teach children is to be elephants, not lions. Becoming mature means learning that you can't always have things your way, and that harming others is unacceptable behaviour. The title Robert Fulham chose for his book, *Everything I Ever Needed to Know, I Learned in Kindergarten*, says it all. So why not make these ordinary, everyday terms the basic language of companies too? Are companies sharing or being selfish? Hurting or helping?

In the same vein, the ingredients of effective communication are good, basic common sense. Be open. Share information. Not just the good stuff, also the bad and the in-between. And not just the boring facts; also the hopes and dreams, the passions and emotions. Talk about the serious things (the so-called hard facts) when they need talking about. But don't forget to share the lighter moments as well.

Very important – don't tell lies (or even bend the truth). And once there is a track record of honesty, trust what the other says. Also, create rituals for dialogue, spaces for talking and listening – the proverbial coffee table chat. Internally, make sure that your environment, health and safety staff sing from the same hymn sheet as line management. So often, a chasm develops between the two, with the environmental brigade perceiving the production guys as unrepentant polluters while the latter view their opposite number as clueless do-gooders who know nothing about production realities, yet have a direct line into the CEO's ear. On the other hand, don't make communication so rigid that it all sounds like propaganda from a central source. Leave some latitude for personal opinions.

There is no shortage of lion companies who mistake 'telling' for 'dialogue' and have been getting backchat from angry stakeholders ever since. McDonald's and Shell have become celebrated examples. When Greenpeace activists published a pamphlet entitled *What's Wrong with McDonald's*, the company was quick to bare its fangs and lash out with its claws by instituting legal action. But McDonald's tough-guy approach bit back – the company found itself in court for 314 days with all its dirty washing being aired for the curious public to see. The resulting tide of discontent from disgruntled stakeholders spawned websites devoted entirely to McDonald's alleged sins on every possible subject.

Shell's fallout with stakeholders over its proposed sinking of the Brent Spar oil platform in the North Sea, as well as its alleged complicity in human rights abuses and environmental impacts in Nigeria, were a wake-up call of note for the company. Faced with widespread consumer boycotts and worldwide anti-Shell activist campaigns, the company was forced to re-examine seriously its old approach of doing business. It shapeshifted its strategy towards adopting the triple bottom line of sustainability and embarked on the most comprehensive stakeholder communication process ever attempted by a multinational. Their public relations effort, reportedly costing $20 million a year, resulted in a programme of public reporting that is today considered by many to be the best in its class. In addition to disclosing a host of externally verified environmental data, they began to listen and share the feedback they were getting from stakeholders. For example, in their 2000 *People, Planet & Profits* report, they quote the input they have received from the United Nations Environment Programme, the World Resources Institute, the World Conservation Union, Harvard Business School and the Ethics Resource Centre.

In addition, they have gone further by recognising that public opinion is as important as 'expert' input. Their 2000 report is liberally sprinkled with quotes from individuals who have responded to the 'Tell Shell' campaign – the good, the bad and the ugly. Senior executives read and discuss these comments as an important indicator of people's feelings on issues of concern to Shell, industry and society at large. Shell is probably still some way off from regaining the trust of many of their stakeholders, but at least they have heard the 'rumble in the jungle' and started to embed the dialogue process into their business.

Fortunately, the next generation of elephant wannabes can learn from McDonald's and Shell's trial-by-fire. Or they can choose the easier route of following in the footsteps of the elephant pioneers that have gone before them. For instance, five years on, The Body Shop's 1997 *Values* report still stands as a world-class benchmark on measuring stakeholder accountability and disclosing stakeholder performance. Similarly, they can take inspiration from Scandinavian companies like Spar Nord Bank (SBN) with their ethical accounting process, or Skandia with their *Intellectual Capital* report, or Electrolux with their environmental reports based on The Natural Step framework. There are also numerous do-it-yourself guides that have emerged in recent years. If taken seriously, for example, the Accountability 1000 standard on Social and Ethical Accounting, Auditing and Reporting and the Global Reporting Initiative's Sustainability Reporting Guidelines could take companies a long way down the road of stakeholder engagement. Beyond these basic frameworks, however, technology-enabled interactive stakeholder feedback and real-time public reporting on the Web are already looming large on the horizon.

Stakeholder communication is one of those areas where many companies are going to be unveiled as lions all dressed up as elephants. The true test of authenticity will not be in the letter of the glossy brochure, but in the spirit of the dialogue. Stakeholders will refine their extrasensory perceptions and develop a sixth sense about which companies are hiding something or bluffing and which are genuinely trying to listen and address the real concerns in good faith. Elephant companies will do what comes naturally – be friendly and caring and compassionate.

6.7 *Services: The genius of Nature*

Products and services will need to shapeshift radically in a sustainable world. It will no longer be acceptable or successful to follow the lion's approach of producing widgets and flogging them to a market brainwashed by advertising, whilst ignoring the damage they cause along the way. The new generation of elephant products and services will focus on adding value over their entire life cycle. In so doing, they will incorporate design characteristics inspired by the genius of Nature. In fact, as you will see later on in this section, many products will become obsolete as they are replaced by 'leased benefits' instead.

The life-cycle approach is one of the rules of the game in an elephant economy. Under this approach, companies are accountable for their products and services from 'cradle to grave'. There are various manifestations of this new philosophy, including life-cycle assessment (LCA), eco-efficiency, supply chain integrity and take-back schemes. LCA is an important tool that can assist companies to quantify the net impacts of their products and services, from raw material sourcing through to final disposal. Although LCA remains a complex and controversial methodology, standards such as ISO 14040-43 can serve as a useful guideline for the uninitiated.

Eco-efficiency is perhaps a less daunting way in which companies can begin to implement life-cycle principles. The term was first used by the Basel-based researchers Schaltegger and Sturm in 1990. But the idea that actions preventing pollution and avoiding waste pay off financially pre-dated this by at least fifteen years. For instance, the US-based consumer goods manufacturer 3M initiated its Pollution Prevention Pays (3P) program in 1975. In the first year, it achieved more than $800 million in savings from 4 000 3P projects. Dow Chemicals launched a similar initiative called Waste Reduction Always Pays (WRAP).

In 1995, Ernst Ulrich von Weizsäcker, Amory B. Lovins and L. Hunter Lovins coined the term *Factor Four* in a book of the same title. The concept refers to doubling resource efficiency (put another way, halving material intensity) and halving waste outputs, thereby effectively reducing the environmental impacts by a factor of four. Seen from a business perspective, this creates the capacity to increase production within a fixed constraint of resources and sinks. The authors cited numerous examples of Factor Four achievements and now others are even promoting the notion of Factor Ten. *Natural Capitalism* is required reading for understanding this exploding new discipline.

Another manifestation of life-cycle principles is the increasing number of product take-back schemes that are being implemented either voluntarily or through legislation. As the word suggests, this involves companies taking back their products at the end of their useful life and either re-using, recycling or disposing of them. In the European Union, for example, five manufacturers – Motorola, Ericsson, Nokia, Alcatel and Panasonic – are jointly implementing voluntary take-back schemes. Rank Xerox is another example: in 1995 alone, the company recovered 80 000 (two thirds) of the photocopiers disposed of in Western Europe, with savings on virgin raw materials exceeding £50 million and the avoidance of disposal costs for over 7 000 tons of material.

One company that has taken the life-cycle principles to their natural conclusion is US carpet manufacturer Interface whose inspiring leader, Ray Anderson, was introduced earlier in the book. Central to Anderson's vision of Interface as a 'restorative company' was the concept of the Evergreen Lease, converting the carpet as a product of material into a product of service. Now known as Evergreen Service Contracts, the programme gives clients the option to lease the services (functionality, colour, design, aesthetics) of a modular carpet system without taking ownership or liability for ongoing maintenance and the ultimate removal for reclamation or recycling at the end of the carpet's useful life. Anderson was able to re-define Interface from being a carpet manufacturer into a provider of sustainable floor-covering services. Surely this product-leasing approach is a glimpse of the future?

This leads us on to the emerging discipline of supply chain integrity. While eco-efficiency, take-back schemes and product leasing are mainly aimed at the environmental elements of life-cycle accountability, supply chain integrity auditing begins to address social impacts as well. Companies like The Body Shop and Traidcraft pioneered the idea of checking the ethical practices of their suppliers and actively engaging in fair trade practices. Following its embarrassing episode of being implicated in using sweatshops, even Nike got the message and began to do audits on labour practices in its own and its suppliers' factories worldwide. In the elephant landscape of the future, scrutiny up and down the supply chain is going to become standard operating procedure.

So these are some tools and techniques that will be useful in shapeshifting products and services. However, the biggest shapeshift probably has less to do with new methods or models, and more to do with inspiration. That is the potential for products and services to be inspired by the genius of Nature. Nature is the ultimate benchmark for a service-oriented system. Every ecological process is highly tuned to the needs of its benefactors, and every species is intimately aware of its connectivity and is constantly adapting to the conditions of its environment. Every detail of the universe, from the macrocosmic to the micro subatomic levels, embodies incredible feats of intelligent design.

There are efficiencies in Nature that are only dreamed about by today's industrial engineers. Nature offers a multitude of lessons for business and an endless supply of inspirational design features for products and services. Already, today's eco-engineers are making design breakthroughs by studying termite hills and prairie dog burrows for improving air-conditioning systems; sharks and owls for cutting down noise pollution from aeroplanes; wasp nests for more robust urban design and construction; octopuses and butterflies for dynamic camouflage technology; leaves for photosynthetic solar energy cells; and lobsters for more mobile extraterrestrial exploration vehicles. The possibilities are endless.

Elephants themselves are a prime example of intelligent design. Their trunks are an inspiration for multifunctionality, serving as hand, nose, mouth, voice and radar all in one. Their ears can detect infrasound as low as 14 hertz and are a highly effective air-conditioning mechanism as well. Their tusks are used for digging, stripping bark and self-defence. Their feet are padded and cushioned to create unbelievable stealth and agility. And their vast wrinkled skin protects them against the ravages of sun, rain, snow and parasites.

Importantly, nature-inspired products and services are usually oriented towards the triple bottom line. It goes without saying that, in Nature, ecological integrity is an in-built system condition: because every output is an input; waste equals food. However, social harmony is also inherent in maintaining viable ecosystems, as Nature relies on symbiotic relationships of mutual interdependence. In addition, due to the efficiencies that Nature has refined over billions of years, its designs are more likely than not to minimise resource consumption and turn waste into by-products. Once again, we are re-emphasising the need to search for new images and metaphors to serve as positive visions of the future. It is clear that we need to shapeshift beyond the Industrial Age which has anyway been a dated symbol for the past four decades. And, while most would agree that we are well into the Information Age, which has the potential to usher in the elephant world of interconnectivity, some are already looking beyond it.

American futurist, Hazel Henderson, is tickling the ivories with a new and catchy tune from the sidelines. "The Information Age is no longer an adequate image of the present, let alone a guide to the future," she says. "It still focuses on hardware technologies, mass production and economic models of efficiency and competition, and is more an extension of industrial ideas and methods than a new stage in human development." Henderson points to a growing realisation by humanity of its dependence on Nature, and more precisely, on light from the sun. Beyond the mushrooming ecological movement and the call for sustainable development, she draws support for her theory from the recent phenomenal growth in leading-edge technologies that do nothing more than attempt to mimic the genius of Nature. Examples of these include artificial intelligence technologies, biotechnologies, energy technologies, and lightwave technologies/phototronics. Reflecting on these developments, Henderson talks about a "repatterning of the exploding Information Age into an emerging Age of Light".

Which metaphor endures in the next fifty years is not so important as the fact that its basic characteristics will reshape the way that companies do business. What is clear to us is that the landscape of our future will be vastly different from the present, and that the ability to understand the complex web of relationships that are woven around and within companies will be critical to surviving and thriving. This is something that will be impossible to achieve if business clings to its self-centred 'drive into the future by looking into the rear-view mirror' approach. The metamorphosis will necessarily require business to assume a more open, compassionate and intuitive identity. This is what corporate responsibility ultimately means: the ability to respond to the needs of stakeholders, to the limits of the Earth, to the impacts of business processes on others, and to the magical potential that is inherent in people and Nature.

7 Sustainable Economics: Shaping a New Landscape

Today's economy is almost exclusively lion habitat. The structures, policies, mechanisms and professions for the most part support lion behaviour – unlimited growth, speculative markets, unfair competition and unchecked concentration of economic power. Yes, the state now has at its disposal antitrust units and monopolies commissions to protect the public interest, and they do intervene. But you only have to look at how mergers and acquisitions have soared over the last twenty years to realise that, apart from one or two notable exceptions that were disallowed, the trend has been irresistible.

This tells you something. It is unreasonable to expect companies to shapeshift without the economy being transformed as well. We need an economy that encourages the emergence of elephant companies who are quite happy to coexist with other companies rather than gobble them up. A sustainable economy is therefore one which ensures the provision of appropriate goods and services to enhance the quality of life of *all* citizens; and done in a way that is socially just and equitable as well as ecologically sustainable and responsible. That is quite a mouthful. However, we are *not* implying by it that some Big Brother should oversee the distribution in accordance with his notion of justice and fairness. Given human nature, the majority of goods and services will invariably end up in his hands. On the other hand, we are urging you not to believe the roars and purrs of politicians and economists who are stuck in the TINA trap – where TINA stands for **T**here **I**s **N**o **A**lternative. Instead, we must embrace the promise of TEMBA – **T**here **E**xist **M**any **B**etter **A**lternatives, some of which are introduced in the sections to follow and all of which preserve freedom of choice. Indeed, certain of the suggestions enhance freedom of choice for the poor.

7.1 *Measures: Tracking the big game*

The issue of a blind devotion to growth was touched on previously as one of the legacies of the lion. This section looks in more detail at the concept of indicators, the limitations of gross domestic product (GDP) as a measure of progress, as well as some of the more elephant-friendly alternatives. The world we live in is exceedingly complex. We use indicators to simplify things. Indicators work in the same way as a map. They are meant to be a guide, a representation of reality, which help us to understand the lie of the land. The scale of the map and what it is trying to measure will determine how accurately and completely it approximates reality.

It is the same with indicators. Some indicators are overarching, global estimates; others are detailed, local measures. Some focus on economic activity; others on social welfare. They help us to understand 'where we're at' and how things have changed over time. Checked against our objectives, indicators tell us whether things are good or bad, better or worse. So far, so good. Except that sometimes we get lazy. In the midst of our information overload, we are tempted to oversimplify. We settle for using a 1:50 000 scale map when we really need a 1:5 000. Or we use a two-dimensional route map when a three-dimensional contour map is called for. This is the main problem with economic indicators today.

GDP is the classic example of a blinkered lion approach to indicators. GDP is a simple and useful measure of economic activity: the sum of all the goods and services produced and sold in a country in a given year. Yet ever since its invention, politicians, multilateral agencies and economists have used

GDP as a proxy measure for progress, welfare and quality of life. As seen through the eyes of an elephant, there are a number of serious limitations to GDP as an indicator today.

The main weakness is that GDP measures the *quantity*, but not the *quality*, of economic growth. For example, if there is a war, an environmental catastrophe or rapid growth in the narcotics trade, more goods and services are sold but society is not better off as a result. In short, GDP makes no distinction between the 'goods' and 'bads' in the economy. GDP also ignores vast areas of economic activity, simply because they are not included in the formal economy. This includes the 'invisible' work performed by households, parents, communities, charities, religious institutions, NGOs and the informal sector. The economic value of these 'free' activities is enormous, yet they go unrecognised. On the other hand, GDP fails to pick up inequity or ethical considerations. It tells us nothing about the conditions under which the goods and services were produced, who is buying them or how the revenues are being distributed. For instance, we don't know how much of economic growth derives from the hands of child labour, or whether bribery and corruption assisted in clinching an extra deal. Yet, if GDP continues to go up, this is interpreted as a signal that 'all is well'.

Finally, GDP fails to capture local conditions. The economy in South Africa may very well be growing nationally, but unemployment and poverty in an urban township could be acute. On the other hand, a rural village in Chile which has a negligible effect on GDP and the official countrywide employment rate may be very much self-sufficient with a high quality of life. One wonders, for instance, what the turnaround in Stutterheim's fortunes – a small town in the Eastern Cape of South Africa whose mayor has transformed it into a thriving small business network – contributed to GDP. Fortunately, the elephant supporters who are critics of GDP have not been without suggestions for improvement. They propose that GDP be turned into a better indicator of overall welfare or quality of life through various adjustments. At the same time separate indicators to supplement GDP should be developed.

The most widely recognised adjusted-GDP measure is the Human Development Index (HDI) produced by the United Nations since 1990. In 1995, the UN also introduced variations of the HDI in the form of the Gender-Related Development Index (GRI) and the Gender Empowerment Measure (GEM), and in 1997 the Human Poverty Index (HPI).These high-profile measures – with components such as life expectancy, education, health, access to basic services, income inequality and long-term unemployment – begin to move us beyond tracking only lion behaviour.

One of the previously mentioned conclusions of the *2000 Human Development Report*, which contains HDI rankings for 1998, is that "the link between economic prosperity and human development is neither automatic nor obvious". For example, while South Africa ranks 49 in GDP per capita out of 173 countries on the basis of purchasing power parity in US dollars (PPP US$), it is ranked much lower down at 103 in terms of its HDI score. Furthermore, South Africa has virtually the same HDI (0.697) as El Salvador (0.696), but more than double the GDP per capita (PPP US$). Conversely, Vietnam and Guinea have similar incomes, but vastly different HDI values (0.671 and 0.394 respectively). Sweden, on the other hand, lies just outside the top twenty at 21 on GDP per capita, but comes in sixth on the HDI.

Another even more comprehensive adjusted-GDP measure is the Index for Sustainable Economic Welfare (ISEW) developed by former World Bank economist Herman Daly and co-author John Cobb. The first ISEW was calculated for the

US and published in their 1989 book *For the Common Good*. The ISEW, as its name suggests, has all the features of an elephant-tracking device with more than twenty factors adjusting for the social and environmental costs of growth. The ISEW has been calculated for nine countries to date comprising Australia, Austria, Chile, Germany, Italy, Netherlands, Sweden, the UK and America. All the countries have displayed the same basic pattern when plotted against GDP: namely that despite ongoing economic growth since the 1950s, the ISEW has slowed, levelled or declined. In other words, although we have become collectively richer if money is used as a yardstick, we are less well off in terms of human wellbeing and development. At some point in the past fifty years, our lifestyle reached a peak and thereafter began to erode on account of the very factor that was supposed to enhance it – industrial growth. Thus, economic expansion no longer translates automatically into a better quality of life.

The Genuine Progress Indicator (GPI), developed by the US public policy research organisation, Redefining Progress, takes a similar approach to the ISEW and reaches similar conclusions. While GDP has more than doubled in America since the 1950s, the GPI shows an upward curve from the early fifties until about 1970 but a gradual decline of roughly 45 per cent since then. The GPI creators conclude that modern economic growth is actually uneconomic – the costs have begun to outweigh the benefits. "Much of what we now call growth of GDP," they say, "is really just one of three things in disguise: fixing blunders and social decay from the past, borrowing resources from the future, or shifting functions from the traditional realm of household and community to the realm of the monetized economy."

The Pilot Environmental Sustainability Index (PESI) is an example of an elephant indicator that seeks to supplement rather than adjust pure economic measures like GDP. The PESI was developed by the World Economic Forum in collaboration with Yale and Columbia Universities, and launched at their annual meeting in Davos, Switzerland in 2000. The PESI has been calculated for 56 economies, with South Africa ranking 43. It is an extremely comprehensive index comprising 64 variables grouped under the following five components: environmental systems, environmental stresses and risks, human vulnerability to environmental impacts, social and institutional capacity and global stewardship.

One of the primary conclusions from the PESI analysis, which was mentioned earlier in the book, is that "there is no clear relationship between a country's observed economic growth rate and its environmental sustainability". Interestingly, however, a correlation does exist between an economy's PESI and its Economic Competitiveness Index. This suggests that economic performance and environmental sustainability are not necessarily trade-offs. Occasionally, the correlation breaks down. For example, while Sweden's Economic Competitiveness Index is almost half that of the United States (0.9 versus 1.6), its PESI score is significantly higher (76 versus 68).

Another facet of elephant-type economics thinking is to encourage local economic activity and community driven self-reliance. Development of community-based economic indicators of welfare and quality of life is of great assistance in this process. National measures provide useful information for national policies, but quality of life is always a local experience. GDP, ISEW and GPI may all be registering an improvement country-wide; but this is not helpful to a local community experiencing job layoffs and increased crime; or living next to a polluting factory; or suffering from dust storms caused by wind blowing off nearby mine dumps.

An example of community indicators is the Quality of Life Index developed by Pierce County, Washington, USA. This benchmark project tracks eighty indicators grouped into nine separate areas of local concern. Tracking the Quality of Life Index between 1989 and 1996 showed an overall improvement of six per cent. The true value of the measure, however, is in its detail. Pierce County discovered that 46 indicators had improved, 26 had declined and eight showed no real change. This kind of localised information empowers the community to tackle those specific areas where quality of life is suffering, enhance those that are stagnant and maintain the improvement in those that are rising.

Over the past hundred years, we have become increasingly aware of the interconnectedness of our global world. A highly complex web of relationships and dynamic forces shape our lives; and yet we still use outdated, simplistic and incomplete measures of progress such as GDP. As futurist Hazel Henderson says, this is "literally like trying to fly a 747 with only one gauge on the instrument panel". Citing another analogy, she says: "Imagine if your doctor, when giving you a check-up, did no more than check your blood pressure." In our fast-paced, information-overloaded society, indicators will become more and more important feedback signals in helping us to make effective decisions. Hence, we can no longer afford to be employing measures that mislead or disguise the real state of our progress. We need to put economics into its proper perspective, as only *one* measure of *one* dimension of human activity with potentially positive and negative impacts on society and the environment. In other words, we need to tag the lion and describe its movements and behaviour accurately. Similarly, we need to tag and track the elephants. By creating more balanced, holistic indicators, economics can once again be made to serve humans and the planet and not the other way round.

7.2 *Externalities: Making the predators pay*

The lion, being focused on its prey, pays no attention to any side effects of its hunting operation. So long as it is successful in its hungry mission. Any casualties along the way are just part of the game of focus, hunt, kill, move on, focus, hunt ... The top brass in the military would call it 'collateral damage'. The elephant, on the other hand, is highly conscious of her surroundings and fellow creatures, and goes out of her way to ensure that no harm comes to them and that her actions have a beneficial spin-off. This analogy introduces the economists' useful notion of 'externalities' or spill-over effects. In the lion economy, companies impose costs on society and Nature without paying for these damages – these are negative externalities. On the other hand, lone elephant companies may make contributions to the community or the ecology without being financially rewarded for these benefits – these are positive externalities.

Let us look, for example, at what happens if we decrease the stock of biodiversity, either by a wetland being drained for development, tropical forests being cleared for agriculture, or a valley being flooded for a hydroelectric power scheme. Each of these new activities has benefits, but these accrue mainly to a single beneficiary (a company) in the form of the revenue generated from the product or service created. However, these activities also have social and environmental costs for which the company does not pay. There may be local externalities such as declining soil fertility, soil erosion and loss of local habitat, as well as global externalities, including the loss of potential scientific discoveries (such as cures for disease), a decrease in carbon sink facilities, impaired capacity for regulating the climate and extinction of natural species. In an elephant economy, the company would be made to foot the bill for these wider costs. There are numerous other examples of environmen-

129

tal and social externalities. The effects on health of passive smoking are a typical negative externality. So is pollution of the water, air or land when these affect a third party without compensation. Other examples are congestion of public areas, noise, the introduction of viruses or diseases, crime and hazardous incidents.

Before sustainability became such a priority, companies as the proverbial kings of the jungle were able to ignore many of their social and environmental externalities. Business saw its task as making products, delivering services and generating profits. Dealing with any unfortunate side effects of this money-making process was, they argued, the responsibility of governments and charity organisations. Today, the situation is vastly different. The sustainability trend is forcing companies to internalise their social and environmental externalities, i.e. account for them in their own books.

Climate change provides excellent examples of the application of economic instruments to promote sustainable commercial activity. Let's talk about the externalities first. Research by the World Health Organisation estimates that a failure to reduce greenhouse gases – the chief source of climate change – to a level 15 per cent below that pertaining in 1990 will result in more than eight million *avoidable* deaths between 2000 and 2020. The deaths will be caused mainly by diseases like malaria brought on by warmer surroundings. In addition, climate change is expected to cause massive damage to property and infrastructure as a result of more severe and unpredictable weather patterns in the decades to come. Agriculture-dependent economies and low-lying coastal cities or island states have the most to lose. According to Dr Andre Dlugolecki, director of the world's sixth largest insurance company, CGNU, damage to property due to global warming is currently rising at 10 per cent a year and could "bankrupt the world" by 2065. So expect hikes in house premiums soon!

As far as the International Energy Agency is concerned, implementing climate change policies could cost the US economy $400 billion in losses in GDP and raise the price of gasoline by 53 per cent, electricity by 86 per cent and residential natural gas by 110 per cent. Moving across the ocean to Australia, anticipated policy reforms in relation to greenhouse gases are predicted to cause a 12 per cent hike in the price of aluminium, A$5 billion of additional costs for the power industry and A$70-350 million in extra costs to the oil refineries. All of these costs, and many more, are indications of a collective externality that energy-hungry industries have imposed on society. The lions have been free to enjoy the spoils of their prowess but have not paid the price for their success; namely the cost of fixing the damage they have caused in the course of the hunt. But not for much longer. The elephants are trumpeting in a new era, one in which economic instruments will force the lions to swallow and digest their externalities.

Economic instruments can take many forms; and the wonderful thing about the economic shapeshifting taking place around climate change is that it is serving to pilot-test many of these flexible instruments. We are seeing, for example, development funds, penalty taxes, incentive subsidies and markets in tradable emission permits being launched in rapid succession. One of the first climate change funds to be launched was the World Bank's Prototype Carbon Fund which finances projects that reduce greenhouse gases. By the end of 2001, it had received $60 million of funding from twenty multinationals and five countries. In Japan, low-interest loans are being offered for energy efficiency investments, while the US through its Climate Change Technology Initiative is introducing energy efficiency tax incentives and research and development subsidies to the tune of $6.3 billion.

In 2001, the UK government introduced a Climate Change Levy (CCL) which is a tax on the industrial use of energy. The CCL will add between five and 10 per cent to industry's fuel bills. However, some energy intensive sectors have been offered up to an 80 per cent discount on the CCL if they agree to sign up to certain minimum improvements in energy efficiency or reductions in emissions. A similar energy tax is being proposed in Germany. Also in 2001, the UK launched the world's first national greenhouse gas Emissions Trading System. Essentially, such a system means that a company which faces exorbitant costs in reducing its emissions to a designated level can buy credits from another company which can reduce its emissions *below* the designated level with relative ease. These credits then allow the purchaser to continue emissions *above* the targeted level for the length of time for which the credits are valid. Nevertheless, the costs associated with this option can still be considerable. Other countries and regions are considering following suit, including Australia, Canada, Denmark, the European Union, New Zealand, Norway and the US. In the US, major firms from the Midwest region are already participating in a pilot scheme known as the Chicago Climate Exchange, following their history of successfully trading other emissions such as sulphur dioxide and nitrogen oxides. The International Energy Agency estimates that $30 billion of greenhouse gas credits will be on the market for trading in 2008. A significant fraction of these will be available to developing countries to trade under the Clean Development Mechanism of the Kyoto Protocol.

Some proactive companies have hedged their bets by doing early trades at discounted prices, qualifying them as elephant drag queens on their way to becoming genuine elephants. Already these deals involve an equivalent reduction in emissions of over 10 million tons of carbon dioxide. Companies like BP Amoco and Shell are preparing for the effects of these economic instruments by implementing internal trading schemes on greenhouse gas emissions. Aidan Murphy, Vice President for Climate Change at Shell International, explains the rationale as follows: "It will change the shape of our energy portfolio and reduce future risk." Moreover, the effect of factoring in carbon prices of $5 and $20 per ton of carbon dioxide generated, he says, "will be to gain us a competitive position compared to other companies as a carbon constrained environment is already a market reality".

Without a doubt, we can learn from this experimental phase of addressing climate change, whereby economic instruments are being used to promote sustainable business practices. There are numerous examples from other fields to build on as well: from taxes on noise levels in the Dutch airline industry to levies on UK landfill waste sites to economic incentives in South Africa for recycling aluminium cans. By instituting measures to promote sustainability which are flexible and market-based, governments are educating the lions of the old economy to become more aware of the external costs of their behaviour (and be accountable for them). One can call this shapeshifting of a kind, but it is not truly converting the lions into elephants. After all, if the incentives were removed, the lions would immediately revert to their old behaviour. What you want is for the lions to *volunteer* to be different, but perhaps this is asking too much.

7.3 *Markets: Taming the casino cats*

Each day, the turnover in the world's financial markets is now in excess of $1.5 trillion. It is at least twenty times more than it was in 1980. The explosive growth of this global casino is largely as a result of introducing two new games: futures and derivatives trading. It all began on the Philadelphia Stock Exchange in 1971 and has escalated to a level where only around two per cent of capital flows are backed by trade in real goods. Even the outlaws of this universe are surreal. In the old days, they used to rob banks and ride off with their satchels stuffed with cash – remember Jesse James and Billy the Kid. The new version is the rogue trader who loses all the bank's money in a few unauthorised transactions. And you don't even see the notes disappearing because it's all done electronically.

Not so long ago, the grave warning of economist John Maynard Keynes echoed loud and clear above the chaotic din of frantic stock-market traders: "When the capital development of a country becomes a by-product of the activities of a casino, the job is likely be ill-done". Modern critic, David Korten, who is author of *When Corporations Rule the World*, calls this phenomenon "de-linking money from value". He argues that capital is being diverted away from long-term productive investment in the 'real economy' in favour of short-term speculative investment in the 'virtual economy'. Keynes and Korten can both be classified as elephants with a keen sense of hearing. They picked up signals of just how real and harmful the effects of this money-making game can be on real people. Furthermore, since the development of expert systems and programmed trading in the 1960s, financial markets have become increasingly depersonalised and automated. High tech means high speed and everybody gets to know the same news at the same time. Gun-slinging traders simply chase the highest margins and returns without any regard for the consequences on local communities, the environment or whole national economies. All in the name of that familiar feline slogan – free trade.

It comes as no surprise that those who are grabbing the lion's share of the benefits from speculative trading are the same ones that have been roaring for greater deregulation of capital flows over the decades. Their selfish tirades have been remarkably successful too, beginning with the creation of the Eurodollar markets and the discontinuation of the gold-dollar fixed exchange system in the 1970s and culminating in their proposal for a Multilateral Agreement on Investment in the late 1990s. Through the calculating lions' eyes of the financial heavyweights, these developments have read like a tale of triumph against government control over money. However, from a social or public perspective – the elephant's point of view – the trend has only served to concentrate power in the hands of an unelected, invisible few with accountability to no one but themselves.

One of the worrying side effects of speculative trading is an increase in the volatility and instability of financial markets. In turn, by making real economies more unpredictable, these roller-coaster fluctuations destroy the livelihoods of small traders and farmers, increase business bankruptcies and disrupt the plans of supposedly sovereign governments to provide a better life for all. The net result of these dizzying effects is a decrease in self-reliance at national, community and individual levels. Ask the Enron pensioners how they feel about having their entire pensions wiped out and having to rely on welfare to survive. Ask any recent visitor to a bookshop in South Africa. The precipitate fall in the Rand has put an ordinary imported paperback beyond the reach of all but the wealthiest customers. Thank heavens this is a locally produced one.

The 'systemic risk' which such financial craziness poses is widely recognised, as an International Banking survey supplement in *The Economist* indicates. So too is the need to tame international financial markets, given the establishment of bodies with imposing titles like the Basle Committee on Banking and Supervision (BCBS), the International Organisation of Securities Commissions (IOSCO), the US Commodity Futures Trading Commission (CFTC) and the Commission for Global Governance Committee on Global Financial Markets (GCFUN).

We even see former super-lions like George Soros (infamous for making over £1 billion from the devaluation of the pound in 1994) showing signs of shapeshifting. Soros is on record as saying that current financial markets will never serve the common good unless controls are introduced. Among other things, he now advocates that "all derivatives traded by banks should be registered with the Bank for International Settlements (BIS) through various national regulatory agencies".

Soros is not alone in trumpeting ideas for change. In 1987, economist James Tobin suggested two possible routes for reform of the international monetary system. Either we have to make currency transactions more costly to reduce capital mobility and speculative exchange rate pressures, an idea derived from Keynes; or there needs to be greater world economic integration, implying eventual monetary union and a World Central Bank. The first approach, which has become known as the 'Tobin tax', was favoured by Tobin and has also become popular among a select group of economists and politicians. Tobin described his proposal as "an internationally uniform tax on all spot conversions of one currency into another, proportional to the size of the transaction", suggesting a charge range of between 0.5 to 1 per cent. Economist Rudi Dornbusch goes further with a recommendation of a cross-border tax on all financial transactions instead of just currency trades. The tax would be collected by the governments concerned.

Subsequently, the United Nations Development Programme (UNDP) commissioned a study by a group of influential economists, which came out in support of a Tobin fee of between 0.05 and 0.25 per cent. This was later endorsed at the UN World Summit on Social Development in Copenhagen in March 1995 by France's President Mitterand, Norway's Prime Minister Bruntland and Denmark's Poul Nyrup Rasmussen. Later that year at the G-7 Summit in Halifax, the idea was given a further boost by Canadian Human Resources Minister Lloyd Axeworthy and UN High Commissioner for Human Rights Jose Ayala Lasso. Nevertheless, despite the support of all these worthy people, the 'Tobin tax' has yet to be enacted.

Those in favour of Tobin's second alternative for reform have proposed an International Currency Unit, to be administered by a World Central Bank and based on an equivalent 'basket' of goods in each country. The value of these baskets in domestic currency would determine relative exchange rates, which would therefore depend on real domestic economic conditions rather than short-term currency movements. Others have called for the coordination of interest-rate policies among the G-3 (the US, the European Union and Japan), thereby enabling countries to pursue their own interest-rate objectives without destabilisation from competing interest-rate policies induced by foreign exchange transmissions and speculation.

Yale University professor and official historian of the UNDP, Ruben Mendez, has proposed a social innovation that may work in conjunction with a currency exchange fee or as an alternative to it. He proposes that a not-for-profit global foreign exchange facility (FXE) should be established to perform foreign currency exchange transactions. It could be set up as a public utility, possibly franchised by a group of governments and the UN and in partnership with the International Monetary Fund and Bank for International Settlements.

GCFUN Commissioner, T. Ross Jackson, on the other hand, has suggested a currency market 'circuit breaker' analogous to the one on Wall Street, whereby trading would be halted if a currency came under speculative attack. This would represent an important social innovation because it would offer national governments and central banks a new domestic macro-management tool to insulate their currencies and economies from attack – without having to raise interest rates and subject their citizens and businesses to the risk of an induced recession.

All of these proposals have elephant traits and sustainability motivations. On the one hand, they are an attempt to reduce the probability of a global financial meltdown, the social and ecological consequences of which are too frightening to contemplate. On the other hand, they are aimed at restoring self-reliance to countries and communities which are adversely affected by repeated financial market shocks, crises, capital flight and general volatility. In the elephant version of a globalised economy, the casino cats will not only be tamed but will be forced to stop chasing their tails and start making a *real* contribution to society.

7.4 *Investments: Channelling the rain water*

On the plains of Africa, water is a precious, life-giving resource – much like investment is to the economies of the world. The elephant seeks to channel water in such a way that all animals can benefit, while the lion jealously guards the pool for himself. One way of using capital flows to make a real contribution to society is by directing them towards the growing tide of sustainability projects. This international elephant-friendly trend – also called ethical investment and the socially responsible investment movement –

broadly comprises the conscious use of investments to achieve social, ethical and environmental objectives as well as to make a reasonable financial return.

The 'sustainability investment' phenomenon can be traced back to the beginnings of the corporate social responsibility movement in the United States in the 1930s. But it only really became visible in the 1970s when church and university groups set up funds, such as the Pax World Fund, to avoid investment in any companies which supported the Vietnam War and the Apartheid regime in South Africa. The trend continued to spread and settled into two basic approaches – shareholder activism and screened investments.

Shareholder activism is where groups of shareholders campaign for changes to what they perceive as the unethical practices of the companies they have a stake in. Often they use the annual general meeting as a platform to lobby for their views and create public awareness. Rio Tinto has been on the wrong end of the stick from such groups for years. In the United States, investors who play an active role in 'shareholder advocacy' of social responsibility issues are estimated to hold assets of $922 billion. That represents sizeable clout to the extent that companies prepare themselves in advance for investors who sponsor or co-sponsor resolutions on social issues. It makes for a more exciting annual general meeting. Screened investments, on the other hand, deliberately exclude any investment in companies associated with oppressive regimes, armaments, animal exploitation, tobacco, gambling, alcohol production and environmental degradation. More and more, screened investments are also using 'positive inclusion' criteria, whereby they actively support investments in companies with a good record in environmental awareness, employee welfare or community involvement. This is an evolving field that has grown to embrace over 300 different criteria, with gun control and opposition to genetically modified food among the more recent issues to be factored in.

After growing steadily throughout the 1970s and 1980s, screened investment took off like a rocket in the 1990s. In the US, sustainability investment funds grew 82 per cent between 1997 and 1999 (about twice the overall growth rate) and reached a total of $2.2 trillion or some 13 per cent of all funds under management. There are now around 200 ethical mutual funds in the US. The growth picture in Canada has been similar though the totals are smaller, while the UK market doubled every three years in the 1990s, reaching almost $5.9 billion in 2001. The spread through Europe has also accelerated with twenty sustainability funds being started every year since 1995 and reaching a total of almost 300 in 2001. They are worth an estimated $2.5 billion. Asia lags behind, but the pattern of growth is the same.

Along with the plethora of ethical investment funds that have been established globally, several indexes have been introduced which further illustrate how ethical investments have gone mainstream. These include the Business in Environment (BiE) Index, the FTSE 4 Good Index, the Dow Jones Sustainability Index and the Tomorrow Top 30 Index. The first two indexes survey listed companies on the London Stock Exchange, while the Dow Jones Sustainability Index covers companies globally with an aggregate market capitalisation exceeding $5 trillion. The Tomorrow Index ranks the thirty companies which appear most frequently in the portfolios of 200 of the world's principal funds which call themselves socially or environmentally responsible.

Sustainability investment funds are not limited to developed countries. In South Africa, for example, there are more than a dozen funds that screen according to social and environmental criteria. They range from the pioneering Community Growth Fund launched in 1992 to the most recent entrant, the Fraters' Earth Equity Fund established in 2001. The spotlight thrown on companies by these funds sometimes brings a rude wake-up call to the cosiness of the boardroom. One fund, for example, downgraded an industrial company and cited the following reasons for doing so: "Appalling relations with the union, doubts about the effectiveness and 'tokenism' of their affirmative action policy, an ineffectual retraining programme, environmental problems, and the re-deployment of white managers as consultants at higher cost".

The natural assumption, especially of the cynical lions, is that these sustainability investment funds must sacrifice financial returns in order to achieve their social and ecological objectives. Indeed, a survey by the UK sustainability fund, NM Conscious Fund, revealed that 87 per cent of the unit owners had bought on the strength of the ethical approach of the fund, whereas seven per cent had done so on the grounds of investment performance. But surprising though it may seem, evidence is mounting that many sustainability investments actually outperform the market. For example, an analysis of the US Domini Social Index of 400 ethically screened companies shows that it marginally but consistently outperformed the Standard & Poors 500 Index over a seven-year period. In 1999, according to Credit Suisse, the twenty largest socially responsible funds averaged returns of five per cent above the benchmark S&P 500 index. And the Dow Jones Sustainability Index has also outperformed the market in its two years of existence. So the business of doing good can be good business too.

According to Russell Sparkes, author of the book *The Ethical Investor*, there are good reasons for this unexpectedly superior performance of sustainability funds. In the first instance, responsible investors are forced to avoid large conglomerates and concentrate on smaller companies, which are more likely to grow faster over time. The exclusion of certain companies on the grounds of moral or environmental repugnance may be an indication of legal action and financial problems to come. At the very least, an ethical approach constrains the investor to target companies with decent housekeeping policies. Lastly, sustainability investment requires a higher level of knowledge about the companies in which a stake could be taken than investment managers normally possess: hence sounder choices are made.

It is important not to lose sight of the wood for the trees, however. What are the 'real returns' of sustainability funds? Their true value lies in their directing money towards the fulfilment of social and environmental goals which usually get underfunded in the marketplace. Their returns therefore are not intended to be short term and may not be astronomical in the longer term. Instead, their legacy may be a better world for future generations to live in. In addition, ethical investment may be building up an important system of checks and balances to counter the unrestrained power of the large, influential companies of the lion economy.

7.5 Money: Extending a helping trunk

One of the fundamental flaws of the lion economy is that unless you are a predator, or lucky enough to be one of the elephants selected by an ethical investor in the previous section, your chances of survival in the open bush are low. You need to be either working for a lion company, or you need to be a foxy entrepreneur. If your social upbringing, your education, your set of beliefs or your economic connection only allows you to eat grass, you can forget it – you're probably dead meat!

The old view of economics is that if only lion companies

are allowed to go about their business without interference, there will be jobs for all – full employment. This being the case, anyone not working deserves to suffer because it means that they are basically lazy or not trying hard enough to learn how to hunt. Hence, it is fitting that they are condemned to a survivalist existence, as somebody has to pick up the crumbs that fall from the lion's table.

The problem is that economic growth is no longer (if it ever was) a guarantee for creating jobs. Jobless economic growth is the new reality. Companies in the US Fortune 500 list, for example, shed literally millions of jobs in the last two decades of the twentieth century. Nor have the foxy entrepreneurs been able to make up the enormous shortfall of jobs, especially in vulnerable developing economies. As a result, there are hundreds of millions of people whose potential is wasting away while they struggle to make ends meet without any source of income.

This type of economic barbarism rubs elephants up the wrong way. It goes against their beliefs about human rights, democracy and ethical behaviour. More than this, it goes against good common sense. Therefore, a pioneering group of elephants are arguing that a fundamental re-perception needs to occur about the way that we structure work and welfare. We have to move our focus from creating employment to creating livelihoods. We have to empower people to put whatever skills and talents they may have to good use. People should not have to spend all their energy and resources on struggling to survive. Nor should they have to wait to be offered a job or to be told that they are economically valuable only when they engage in productive work for someone else in the private or public sector.

But how would a more universal model of empowerment be achieved? There are no easy answers or ready-made solutions to this one. The shapeshifting has yet to occur. We have to de-link ourselves from the notions of classical western economics and come up with ideas from other sources. In this vein, there are three powerful avenues that merit further explanation. The first two have been around for some time and the third is beguiling in its simplicity. All three have the potential to start stretching our snouts into trunks and our fangs into tusks. They are: barter networks, parallel currencies and the basic income grant.

Barter networks are one way to address the apparent scarcity of money. Most estimates place the value of bartering at 10 to 20 per cent of world trade today. And much of this is made up of highly sophisticated transactions. In the US, there are information networks operating barter systems worth more than $7.5 billion a year. Although they have their limitations, barter networks have great potential for empowering communities that are cash-poor. One inspiring example is called Adopt-A-Neighbour, a scheme which Lawrence Snell, a former insurance consultant, coordinates in Cape Town, South Africa. He describes the seed for the idea as follows: "As a child growing up in the informal settlement of Elsies River (after being evicted by the government from the suburb of Vasco), I was exposed to the *kanalah* system of empowerment among the Moslem community. *Kanalah* means much more than literally 'please'; it's something about doing things for Allah. This system is chore-related and not about monetary value." Today, Adopt-A-Neighbour coordinates a barter exchange system among its local Strandfontein community of 4 000 families. The barter network's philosophy just about sums it up: their mission is 'helping you achieve sustained, fulfilled living'; their vision is 'when you need help, we are all the help you need'; their goal is to answer the question 'how may we help you?' successfully; and their currency is 'goodwill', which is not measurable.

The poverty-stricken city of Curitiba in Brazil is another example of the creative use of bartering. In the 1990s, the city faced two problems: an underutilised public transport system and mounting piles of garbage in the streets. So the mayor invented a new system where he would give one bus token in return for each bag of pre-sorted garbage delivered. This extended to giving students notebooks in exchange for the garbage. Building on the success of this initial experiment, Curitiba managed to complete numerous public projects for which there was no official budget, and thereby improved the quality of life of its citizens drastically.

Parallel currencies are simply a more flexible form of barter exchange system. The basic idea, which is to have local currencies running in parallel with the official national monetary system, is not as new as some might think. Among the first examples of this phenomenon are the 'Guernsey Island notes' issued in 1819, Robert Owen's 'National Equitable Labour Exchanges' in London and Birmingham, Joseph Warren's 'Time notes' in Cincinnati in the 1830s, and Silvio Gesell's 'stamp script money' in the Austrian town of Wörgl during the years of the Great Depression in the 1930s. In fact, the Depression subsequently caused hundreds of European and North American cities to issue their own money in order to speed up recovery. One of the initiatives to endure was Switzerland's 'WIR' script – a currency exclusive to WIR-Messen, a member-owned cooperative exchange system started in 1946. By the mid-1990s the cooperative comprised thousands of members and was responsible for 19.7 million Swiss Francs equivalent of trade.

Today, one of the most popular and enduring parallel currency systems is LETS. It stands for the Local Exchange Trading System. LETS was first established by Michael Linton in 1983 when his rural community in British Columbia,

Canada, was devastated by an economic recession. The system allows members to trade both goods and services, using a combination of conventional currency and community-created credit called 'Green dollars'. Members' balances are kept on a central computer programme and are updated on a daily basis. LETS has since spread to other countries including the US, England, New Zealand and Australia.

In developing countries, there are numerous variations on the LETS theme: the *Bia* currency in the Kud Chum district in Yasothon, Thailand; the *Tlaloc* currency in the neighborhood of Colonia Tlaxpana, Mexico; the *Compromisos* of Toctiuco in Quito, Ecuador; and the *Bons de Travail* of the Grand-Yoff district of Senegal's capital, Dakar. Hazel Henderson claims that a similar type of 'local currency' rationale was behind China's record run of domestic growth. Transactions between Chinese citizens were all done using 'village money' or the *renminbi*, which was not easily convertible to the *yuan* or to the Foreign Exchange Certificates issued to visitors. Thus, the bulk of income generated internally did not leak out of the country.

LETS schemes and other parallel currencies display all the essential features of money: they are a means of exchange, a unit of value, a store of worth, a form of organisation and a relationship of trust. Importantly, however, they tackle the problem of low local liquidity since they do not require participants in the scheme to have a formal job, an income stream or a stock of money to get themselves started. The genius of parallel currencies is that money is only created by the act of goods or services being exchanged. Hence, they don't lead to inflation but spread wealth to where it is most needed in a community.

Before moving on to the third idea, one of us has for several years proposed a variation of LETS: the establishment of local stock exchanges in each province of South Africa so that local venture capital finds its way into local businesses. It makes sense for investors to be able to visit the entrepreneurial ventures they invest in and inspect the books. This they can only do if they live in the neighbourhood and get acquainted with the owners of the businesses. The shame at the moment is that the bulk of any savings that a community does manage to accumulate usually finds it way via the local branch of the banks into the big city projects – because the latter are regarded by the bank's head office as a safer bet. Gone are the days when bank managers were regarded as prominent leaders in the community playing the crucial role of extending credit to farmers and tradesmen, particularly when they had fallen on hard times. Today most bank managers are rotated (if they still exist) so they never get to know their clients; and all loan requests are handled centrally by bureaucrats and computers with the consequence that only your assets – and not your character – count in obtaining a loan. And who wants an umbrella in the sunshine?

The final jumbo-sized concept for delinking survival and jobs is the institution of a Basic Citizen's Income which has been promoted by the London-based New Economics Foundation for a decade now, and is gaining support worldwide. In South Africa, following the 1998 Job Summit, the leading trade union federation COSATU has been campaigning for the implementation of a Basic Income Grant (BIG). The details are being extensively researched by its Economic Policy Research Institute. The idea is that every citizen should be entitled to a minimal annual grant that will keep him or her just above the poverty datum line. South African economist Margaret Legum explains the BIG concept as follows: "All nationals would be entitled to a BIG, from the cradle to the grave. It would not be means tested. It is not a 'safety net' for losers. It would be enough

147

to supply basic needs but not enough to discourage people from working for money. It would be less for children and more for old people over working age. It would be given out automatically, like a pension or child allowance. It would require no bureaucracy to administer. It could be financed in a number of ways, mainly through one of the alternative taxes, such as eco-taxes."

She explains that a BIG would enable all citizens to have a stake in the economy. It would boost purchasing power for everyone, hence it would stimulate a market for local enterprise. It would enable some essential work, like childcare, to be done full-time. Introducing a BIG would prevent extreme labour exploitation, since people would not be desperate enough to accept appalling conditions of work. It would also end the extreme poverty and desperation that undoubtedly fuels crime. And it would put an end to the cramping humiliation of the fear of starvation.

All of these ideas – barter exchange networks, parallel currencies and the BIG concept – are attempts to release the masses of poor and unemployed people from the claws of the lion economy that ties survival to formal, money-paying jobs. We are not suggesting that these are the best, or the only, ways to solve the problem of community economic empowerment. They are, however, illustrations of how we can begin shapeshifting towards an elephant economy that successfully includes all people and cares for them, rather than cutting them off and throwing them on the lion's trashheap.

7.6 Banking: Financing a healthy herd

We have already touched on banking twice in this book, but the industry as a whole deserves a separate section. Lions say that 'money makes the world go round' and then turn the saying into a self-fulfilling prophecy by controlling the purse strings. It is one of the great ironies of the feline economy that those who most desperately need money are denied it, or made to pay an exorbitant price to get it. Most banks consider the poor as 'unbankable' and focus their appetites on 'high net worth' individuals. The latter are usually shareholders as well, so they don't ask questions about where the bank invests its money as long as it hunts down the best financial returns. In these circumstances, the bank is an exclusive preserve for lions with the lion king (the CEO) occasionally gracing the front page of the financial press to report another significant increase in earnings per share.

In the elephant economy, however, equitable access to finance is high on the list of priorities, as is ensuring that the banks invest their money in sustainable activities. An example of financing a healthy herd is the growth of the community development banks in the USA. They have adopted the express objective of providing financial services and investment to marginalised communities in order to aid their upliftment. These banks have financed over $2.5 billion worth of community economic development, with the five largest having made loans in excess of $400 million since their inception.

The South Shore Bank of Chicago is a classic example, the heartening story of which has been featured by the *Harvard Business Review*. Back in the 1960s, some of its employees were bankers by day and community volunteers by night. They would have deep discussions at the Eagle Bar about the problems of inner cities and what to do about them. One of these 'idealists' took over the leadership of the bank in 1973 in a bid to save it from closing and to prove that a commercial bank could be a vehicle for regenerating impoverished communities. The bank not only survived, but has since lent more than $130 million to 7 000 local business people with a 98 per cent repayment rate (the same rate of repayment has been achieved by the Grameen Bank in Bangladesh). They have also trained more than 2 200 people, found jobs for another 2 700, built upwards of 9 000 housing units and disbursed more than $1 million in low-interest energy conservation loans. And all this has happened in a community where one fifth of the population lives below the poverty line. South Shore talks about the secret of its success being a return to "old-fashioned banking" in which "banks have local areas and they owe those areas service".

Social banks are the European equivalent of America's community development banks. Their services are intentionally aligned with social and ecological goals and projects. As a sector, these banks are estimated to have financed more than 5 000 'social economy' projects by investing in excess of $100 million. To understand what is meant by social economy, we can look to the example of Triodos Bank. Triodos is a European bank that gives financial support only to "projects and enterprises which create social and environmental value". They operate in fields such as renewable energy, social housing, complementary health care, fair trade, organic food and farming and social business – all areas which are traditionally underfunded. The beauty of their system is that, as an elephant-friendly bank depositor, you have the choice as to what human or ecological initiative you wish your money to be directed towards in the form of a loan. You may also choose to pass on an interest rate 'discount' to the prospective projects you are supporting, by requesting a lower interest rate on your savings. Triodos also finances fair trade and microcredit organisations in developing countries.

Another issue that concerns sensitive elephant types is the potentially perverse effects of interest on the most vulnerable sections of the population. While charging interest on loans dates back more than 4 000 years, so do critiques of its negative impacts. Often the problem arises where destitute borrowers fall prey to loan sharks who charge exorbitant interest rates, thus setting off a downward spiral into the so-called 'debt trap'. This practice of excessive interest is the 'usury' that most of the world's religions have condemned since antiquity. Often, the hidden poison that kills borrowers is not the rate itself, but the fact that it is compounded over time – in other words, charged not only on the original loan sum, but on accumulated interest as well. This has the effect of institutionalising exponential growth of interest rates. To illustrate the potentially devastating effect of this creeping interest, one penny of debt incurred at the birth of Jesus Christ with a compound annual interest rate of five per cent would have grown to the cost of one ball of gold equal to the weight of the Earth by 1466. If repaid in full in 1990, the sum would have purchased 2 200 billion of such balls of gold.

One of the most visible and tragic examples of the casualties of the compound interest trap is the Third World debt crisis. According to the United Nations, at the height of the crisis in the late 1980s the $1.5 trillion in debt repayments by developing countries was three times greater than the original amount owed in 1980. Despite these repayments and more since, the total debt of developing countries is still estimated to stand at more than $1 trillion. Indeed, more money is flowing out of developing countries to service the debt than is being pumped in through international aid. A more effective treadmill could not be devised.

Even though we mentioned the problem of the discount rate at the beginning of Chapter 5, it bears repetition here. Discounting is really the opposite of compounding. Just as a penny today gets unimaginably large when compounded over a long period of time into the future, so a treasure of a million pounds received in a hundred years time appears to be worth a trifling amount now after being discounted. Hence, if the return on keeping a natural resource or investing in a social project happens to be long term, it makes 'economic sense' to exploit that resource now or cancel the project in order to invest the money elsewhere. This theoretically leads to 'economically rational extinction or depletion', an absurdity which ecological economists Daly and Cobb lay bare by asking "when to kill the goose which lays the golden egg?"

German Professor Margrit Kennedy also argues that interest is a key component of pricing. She calculates, for instance, that around 50 per cent of the prices paid on basic goods and services in Germany are hidden interest costs, paid at each step of the production process. According to this argument, a hike in interest rates will directly add to 'cost-push' inflation (negating the dampening effect on 'demand-pull' inflation). She also shows that the growth in national interest payments in Germany is outstripping the growth in gross national product. Finally, she claims that interest causes income to 'trickle up', citing the evidence that the poorest 10 per cent of German households pay out net interest every year while the richest 10 per cent receive net interest. "No wonder", she says, "the rich are getting richer at the expense of the poor."

In reviewing these criticisms of banking and interest, we are not suggesting that an elephant economy will wipe out either, or should wish to. However, ways will have to be found to counteract the negative effects of interest and turn financial institutions into forces for positive change. After all, money is the only commodity where the price you pay is higher the poorer you are. Imagine going into a shop to buy some bread. You ask the owner the price and he replies:

"How much are you worth?" If you demonstrate that it is *your* new Mercedes that is parked outside his shop, he gives you a fat discount. If, on the other hand, you are unconvincing about your wealth, he charges you double the normal price. Is that justice? Yet in the world of credit, that is precisely what happens on the grounds of the greater the risk, the greater the reward that the bank expects. So it all depends which side of the coin you are looking at: the lion's head or the elephant's head.

One of the schools of economics that may have the most to contribute to the shapeshifting of financial institutions is Islamic economics. Since the Islamic tradition embodies serious concerns about the negative distributive justice and equity effects of financial interest, Moslems have gone a long way towards exploring alternative institutional mechanisms collectively called 'Islamic banking'. The specific methods for implementing Islamic banking have centred around equity-based approaches. For example, *Mudarabah* is essentially a joint venture between the bank and a partner with both contributing to the capital of the project and sharing the profit or loss. Another approach, *Musharakah*, requires that all the capital for an investment is provided by the bank in return for a predetermined share of the profit or loss of the business undertaking.

The emphasis in the Islamic banking approach is, therefore, very much one of risk-sharing between lenders and borrowers. This stands in contrast to the Western banking principle of the borrowers being required to pay fixed interest regardless of the success or failure of their business venture. So let's be innovative. Why not have a lower rate of interest that serves as a floor but is topped up by a profit-sharing arrangement which becomes the 'premium' payable for the extra risk? Whatever actual mechanisms emerge from the shapeshifting, we can be sure that financial institutions of tomorrow will no longer be the self-serving 'kitty' of well-to-do lions. The rest of the jungle wants a share of the action.

7.7 Trade: Learning to play fair

In the present era of globalisation, it is a sacrilege to criticise unrestricted free trade when in the company of the pride. Somehow, questioning free trade is equated with being antidemocratic, pro-communist and an all-round sour-grapes loser. And yet evidence of the negative impacts of trade on vulnerable communities, small economies and fragile environments is precisely why elephant thinkers *do* question deregulated free trade. These are the very issues that rumble through the demonstrations that now tag every meeting of the council of supreme lion countries. These disgruntled herds of protesters argue that global trade today is neither free nor fair.

If we look back, the concept of global free trade has its roots in the Bretton Woods conference of 1944. It was one of the main visions of the proposed International Trade Organisation (ITO). As it turned out, the General Agreement on Tariffs and Trade (GATT) signed in 1947 was the only aspect of the ITO to be ratified. Various constraints that were originally designed to regulate the pure trade aspect of the envisaged global economic system were left out. Today GATT is enshrined in the World Trade Organisation (WTO), which continues the crusade for unrestricted trade.

The critics of globalisation cite various reasons for their discontent. The prime argument is that such an environment leads companies to seek out investment destinations with the least number of obstacles to profit-making. The end result is what US ecological economist and author Herman Daly calls 'standards lowering competition' and others have called 'the race to the bottom'. In other words, lion

154

companies will locate in countries with minimal controls on working conditions and negligible environmental protection in order to save on costs that higher standards elsewhere would impose. To borrow the economists' jargon, why internalise externalities if no one is forcing you to?

Another criticism is that trade between parties of unequal strength seldom results in an equitable exchange. How can developed lion economies of the industrialised world claim to be on 'a level playing field' with struggling developing countries reeling under debt and social upheaval? Indeed, how can America and Europe justify protecting their farmers when developing countries are not permitted to protect theirs (sounds like affirmative action in reverse)? Or at a corporate level, is it reasonable to expect local micro-enterprises to face up against powerful multinational companies and compete 'on equal terms'? The elephant economy seeks to redress power imbalances. And there are no more glaring contrasts than in the area of global trade. Competition means that the strong win and the weak lose. So guess who has gained the lion's share of the benefits of globalisation? America! The strongest and richest lion in the first place. No wonder they want the system to continue. Elephants are quick to point out that the WTO itself is undemocratic, despite the recent inclusion of more developing country members. How can that organisation make decisions which affect the lives of billions of people without being subject to any governing body other than itself and lacking proper channels for input and influence by its stakeholders? Even the International Labour Organisation was unsuccessful in its attempts to have a social clause included in the WTO constitution. To many elephants, therefore, it smacks of a self-serving gentlemen's leo club.

Elephants wishing to shapeshift global trade towards something more sustainable have led the charge with a countermovement consisting of a network of 'alternative trade organisations' (ATOs) that strive to promote *fairness* in trade. They do this by agreeing on certain minimum standards and ethical practices which have the welfare of those parties affected (and usually marginalised) by the global trade process as their primary focus. In Europe, this has resulted in the establishment of more than 2 500 'fair trade shops' which exclusively stock products that have been subject to this careful screening process. The UK has been particularly proactive in promoting fair trade through organisations like Traidcraft, Oxfam Activities, Teacraft and TWIN Trading. As an example of their success and impact, Traidcraft has a 2 000 strong voluntary sales staff and has managed to get its tea and coffee products stocked by national retail supermarket chains like Sainsbury's.

The Body Shop's 'Trade Not Aid' initiative took the idea of fair trade and turned it into its international trading policy. Among the principles behind Trade Not Aid were that The Body Shop utilised traditional skills and materials; provided long-term commitments to all community projects of this nature; and encouraged small-scale businesses that could be easily duplicated. Because fair trade became something of a mission for The Body Shop, they actively sought out trade relationships with communities in Third World countries including India, Burkina Faso, Malaysia, Nepal, the Philippines and Kenya. The Body Shop founder, Anita Roddick, sums up their fair trade experience as "the ability to work in partnership with communities and to figure out what they truly need. It is the process of helping people find the right tools, and the right approach, to develop themselves". It is not, she emphasises, simply buying goods for money, or dishing out things we assume people want, or imposing blueprint-type solutions on a complete population. More than anything, fair trade centres around paying attention to human relationships and addressing the particular situation that each counterparty finds itself in.

Fair trade organisations are not limited to First World countries. One of the best examples of an ATO is South Africa's Cape Town-based Triple Trust Organisation. As the name suggests, it was originally established to provide three services: to assist people from township communities to obtain business skills training; to open up access to capital for those who had successfully completed their courses; and to create marketing links which channel income from the pockets of First World customers into the coffers of Third World entrepreneurs. In the last regard, Triple Trust Investments has taken a significant stake in a company called *www.buysouthafricaonline.com*. A recent winner of the 2002 Development Marketplace Innovation Competition of the World Bank, the company has developed a web-based system for small manufacturers to deal directly with the end-consumers of their products. By streamlining the supply chain, small traders in South Africa obtain a fairer share of the final sale price. The company has even addressed the digital divide by enabling remote entrepreneurs to receive their orders automatically by 'sms' on a cellphone, thereby bypassing the need for expensive computer equipment and training.

Another example of an ATO is Fair Trade in Tourism South Africa, which was set up in 1998 as part of an international fair trade network for the tourism industry. The criteria for registering with the organisation reveal the elephant values that underlie the initiative: fair share, democracy, respect for human rights, culture and environment, reliability, transparency and sustainability. It runs on similar lines to an international network called the Ethical Trading Initiative whose membership includes companies, trade unions and NGOs. The corporates in this case are primarily UK retailers, such as The Body Shop, Sainsbury's, Levi Strauss, Marks and Spencer, Safeway Stores and Tesco.

Another dimension of the fair trade philosophy is to be conscious of the benefits of keeping trade local. Even the great economist Keynes acknowledged this when he said: "I sympathise, therefore, with those who would minimise, rather than those who would maximise, economic entanglement between nations. Ideas, knowledge, art, hospitality, travel – these are the things which should of their nature be international. But let goods be homespun whenever it is reasonably and conveniently possible; and, above all, let finance be primarily national."

What Keynes was getting at is that local trade is good for local economies. Not that we should be trying to restrict people's choice. However, keeping money circulating in a given community, or country, is a powerful force in improving the welfare of that community or nation's people. We also know that local trade can avoid the environmental impacts associated with the transportation and packaging of globally traded goods. Therefore, buy-local campaigns like Proudly South African and its counterparts around the world are elephant-friendly initiatives that deserve our encouragement and support.

At the moment, fair trade is just a seed which has had limited exposure and application, but it is nevertheless worth nurturing. As we shapeshift towards an elephant economy, fair trade criteria will become embedded in the practices of all world-class companies. Tools like social auditing and accounting and supplier certification schemes related to various international social, ethical and environmental standards will assist them. And combined with other sustainable economy initiatives, fair trade practices will help to restore some measure of equity and justice into our present conquest-oriented, winner-takes-all international trading system.

8 The Future: Elephants in the Mist

Believe it or not, many cultures have linked elephants with the clouds; some myths even credit elephants with creating the clouds. This is probably because of their comparable size and colour and shape in thundery weather; but there may be symbolic elements as well. Clouds represent the mist that separates the formed worlds from the unformed. Clouds are also forever changing, forever shapeshifting. So it is also not surprising that elephants are associated with prophecy and divination. Add to this the belief in elephants' great memory and wisdom and we have a fitting symbol for our final speculations about the misty future of sustainable business in a shapeshifted world.

Dare one of us say it, but an excellent crystal ball to use when gazing into the future is scenario planning, using the 'foxy matrix' developed in *The Mind of a Fox* (co-authored by Chantell Ilbury and Clem Sunter). The four quadrants of the matrix move our thinking from (1) Rules of the game, to (2) Key uncertainties and scenarios, to (3) Options, and finally (4) Decisions. These will be explored now using the lion and elephant themes of the book.

8.1 *Rules of the game*

The rules of the game are the conditions that we are fairly certain will apply within the foreseeable future. They govern our behaviour and up to a point are beyond our control. Unlike the rules of sport which are conveniently written down in a rule book somewhere, the rules of business are normally unwritten. At times, they are subject to intense debate – particularly when they change, as they are doing at the moment. However, there are certain rules that never change, such as the moral rules of the game. Many lion companies either ignore or fail to understand that business is as subject to the moral rules as an individual is. Nor are they sensitive to those changes in the rules which are taking place as a result of alterations in the environment around them.

We have identified seven rules of the game that underpin the world that is emerging through the mists of time. These are: (1) Spaceship Earth; (2) the demographic multipliers; (3) pervasive poverty, growing resentment; (4) declining ecosystems; (5) a techno-scientific boom; (6) the networked planet; and (7) a renaissance in values.

8.1.1 *Spaceship Earth*

Recalling Kenneth Boulding's 1960s metaphor, we live within an insular planetary system. The only external input is the sun's radiation. To all intents and purposes, nothing comes in and nothing leaves. There is no backup store of resources to tap into once our planet is all used up. And there is no 'away' for the waste and pollution that we create. We can try to hide it by burying it or diluting it, but it doesn't disappear; it just accumulates. For even with our technological wizardry, we cannot replicate the planet's ingenious processes. Up till now, this rule hasn't been a problem. We've got away with ignoring it because for most of the Earth's history the population has been relatively small and only a small proportion of that population has consumed resources at a rate which might cause a problem.

Now, Spaceship Earth is what we would call a 'show stopper'. It is literally a 'killer concern' because, by ignoring this rule, we are in danger of killing ourselves off as a species on this planet. The planet will survive, by the way. This may sound overly melodramatic but it is pure, measurable science: we are slowly poisoning ourselves on the one hand, and threatening the delicate equilibrium of various ecosystems on which we depend on the other. More about this in the key uncertainties.

8.1.2 *The demographic multipliers*

Population has a double whammy effect as a rule of the game. Obviously, a growing population puts more strain on limited resources, such as the environment, food and habitat. And, even with the most optimistic projections on declining fertility rates, the latent population growth that is already 'in the pipeline' will almost certainly result in a doubling of today's six billion people. That would be challenge enough for our Spaceship Earth, but it is only the first multiplier.

The second multiplier is tied up with the industrial lifestyle which developing countries are seeking to emulate, and which is highly resource-intensive and extremely unhealthy, wasteful and polluting. What would happen if the one million pounds of annual waste generated by each American citizen were multiplied by six billion as opposed to 300 million? Or if on the same basis we extrapolated the $100 billion that America spends to combat the harmful effects of air pollution, or the $50 billion in health costs associated with their fast-food diet? Quite simply, if every country adopts these lifestyles, the environmental and social impacts will be catastrophic. The crazy thing is that America has to rely on the rest of the world *not* catching up with it in order to continue with the wasteful lifestyle to which it has grown accustomed.

8.1.3 *Pervasive poverty, growing resentment*

Poverty is a crisis of global proportions. Three billion people still live on less than $2 a day, while more than one billion do not have access to proper food or clean water. According to the United Nations, worldwide poverty has got worse not better over the past fifty years. That's in absolute terms. Relatively speaking, the gap between the 'haves' and the 'have-nots' is also widening, as we alluded to earlier. And being a complex issue, the problem is not going to go away at any time soon. For decades to come, poverty will remain the single biggest threat to social sustainability.

Poverty acts like a cancer in the human society: it eats away at the body from the inside out; there is no simple cure; and by the time it is usually recognised as a threat, it is already too late. Our current belief in 'trickle down' economics is like an ineffective, superstitious placebo. It may make us feel better for a while, but it hasn't rooted out the cause. It's as if we naively believe that if the privileged few keep eating ice-cream which happens to taste great, the good feeling will eventually spread to the less fortunate masses and just melt away the cancer. In practice, the reverse is happening. With the advent of mass media, the poor now know what they're missing out on and a sense of relative deprivation is spreading out like a shock wave. Accompanying the resentment is something to which we refer later on: the access to weapons of mass destruction which the poor increasingly have. Combined with religious fervour, this whole mixture becomes pretty potent.

8.1.4 Declining ecosystems

Some of the facts previously mentioned in the book bear repeating here: we have lost over ten per cent of the species that were living a few hundred years ago; the Earth is losing an estimated three or more species per hour, a rate one hundred to one thousand times greater than the average over the preceding hundreds of millennia; and conservation biologists are predicting that half of the diversity of life will be lost in the next century if the present rates of habitat destruction and disturbance continue.

Need more facts? In the past fifty years, the world has lost a quarter of its topsoil and a third of its forest cover. At present rates of destruction, we will lose 70 per cent of the world's coral reefs, host to a quarter of marine life, in our lifetime. In the past three decades, one third of the planet's natural resources has been consumed. We are losing freshwater ecosystems at the rate of six per cent a year, marine ecosystems at four per cent a year. At the same time, we are starting to wreak havoc with our climate system. There is no longer any serious scientific dispute that things are getting worse, even in the ten years since the Rio Earth Summit of 1992.

On the other hand, a very powerful driving force behind modern business was introduced unwittingly by Peter Drucker, the American guru, when he invented 'management by objectives' in the middle part of the last century. Nowadays, MBO as it is known is at the centre of all strategic, operational and budgetary processes. You set objectives and then you measure your performance against those objectives, whether they are financial ones, production ones, marketing ones, etc. Because we naturally aspire to do better in the eyes of the people we fear and respect (for underlings read bosses, for bosses shareholders) our objectives tend to reflect this. We select targets which will lower costs, raise production and produce more profit. Continuous improvement is the Zeitgeist. Nobody budgets lower profit unless it is due to factors beyond his or her control. Thus, while Drucker himself may be an open-minded and balanced individual, his product – MBO – has entrenched a culture of 'more', just when we need a culture of 'less' according to this rule of the game.

Worse still, MBO creates the impression that the future is certain and management is in control. The objectives must be attained whatever the future has in store. It's rather like the pilots of an airliner having a flight plan and no radar system to indicate that the flight plan should be changed in the event of bad weather ahead. The facts we have quoted under this heading show that some really bad weather is about to be encountered if we don't change course immediately.

8.1.5 *The techno-scientific boom*

The pace of scientific discovery and technological innovation shows no signs of abating. Whether it is mapping the human genome, building artificial intelligence machines, or cloning animal life, each new revelation sparks a whole industry of possibilities. We just need to look at how many mainstream career options today did not exist fifty years ago: VCR/mobile phone design and engineering, computer science, biotechnology, corporate environmental management, microelectronics, website design, contamination remediation – the list could go on and on.

In our struggle to cope with the whirlwind of change that surrounds us, we should resist the temptation to react like the Luddites of old – those bands of English artisans bent on destroying machinery in the early nineteenth century in the belief that all new technology was evil. The information technology revolution has reshaped our world forever; and wave upon wave of scientific breakthroughs in the twenty-first century will continue to toss and tumble us about until we learn to surf each new change. The hope is that technological advance can create environmentally-friendly substitutes in the fields of materials and energy, so vital for people to improve their standard of living within the constraints of inhabiting Spaceship Earth.

8.1.6 *The networked planet*

Hand in hand with the spread of democracy around the globe, the planet has become a world wide web. The so-called information superhighway is a vast network of fibre-optic cables, radio waves, microwaves and satellite signals. Whether you are standing on the top of Mount Kilimanjaro or at the bottom of the Grand Canyon, a little black box called a cellphone can connect you with anyone else on Earth. Or a web-cam can teleport someone live into your home for a chat, as if he or she were sitting across the coffee table from you.

This is the fishbowl reality of today's world – real-time, larger than life news about anything, anywhere; near-instantaneous duplication and dissemination of information; and cyber-societies of virtual relationships between like-minded people scattered around the globe. Commit any corporate sins against sustainability and there is nowhere to run, and nowhere to hide. On the other hand, if you are one person trying to make your voice heard, just plug into the Internet and go on a surfing safari. On the way, you will make lots of friends and learn all you need to know to make a difference collectively.

8.1.7 *A renaissance in values*

The social and environmental movements that have gained momentum over the past five decades are more than just a collection of events, or a passing phase of human introspection. In the process, our global society has been changing at its very core. We have seen the bubbling up of age-old values – like honesty and selflessness and compassion – in a shift that may prove with hindsight to be as profound as the triumph of democratic principles over dictatorial monarchy, or civil freedom over human slavery.

In essence, what the sustainability trend is in the process of doing is rending the veil on the hypocrisy of today's political institutions, economic ideologies, and business organisations, all of which exist within societies that proclaim the virtues of one or more of the great religious or spiritual traditions of the world. As in the children's parable of Snow White, the shift in values now under way in society is acting like that 'mirror, mirror on the wall' which sees beyond superficial appearances (like political speeches, economic mumbo-jumbo, and corporate values statements), and judges character solely on the basis of the actions of the person or institution concerned. We have moved from 'tell me' to 'show me'.

8.2 *Key uncertainties*

Key uncertainties are those variables that could go one way or the other; they are the pivotal points on which the future swivels. It is critical that we explore these because often their outcome depends partially on our choices and actions over the short term as well as longer term factors beyond our control. However, it is just as crucial to realise that the future contains 'unknown unknowns'. These wild cards come out of the blue and can make a huge difference. In other words, beware of placing too much faith in our powers of foresight. The future can always surprise us.

With the qualification just expressed in mind, we have identified seven key uncertainties: (1) willingness to share power; (2) the direction of innovation; (3) economic and trade policy developments; (4) political maturity; (5) the rate of environmental decline; (6) social unrest; and (7) lifestyle choices.

8.2.1 *Willingness to share power*

One of the things that made South Africa's transition to democracy so remarkable was that F. W. de Klerk was prepared to surrender his position of supreme power as president in the interests of the country's future. He had the strategic insight to realise that holding onto power in a pariah state would, sooner or later, result in civil war and unnecessary bloodshed. The temporary power-sharing arrangement negotiated between De Klerk and Nelson Mandela was the only sane solution, but it took great courage and vision to let go of control and begin to trust those formerly regarded as enemies.

Businesses face the same dilemma. Either they continue to cling to their already awesome power and dominance in the world at the expense of future environmental and social sustainability; or they have the wisdom to start sharing that power – with Third World countries, with local communities, with environmental interest groups, and so on. The key uncertainty is the extent to which lion-minded businesses will realise that their current winner-takes-all course is a path towards self-destruction, and that power sharing is the only sustainable way forward. Equally, a key uncertainty overhangs the attitude of the West – particularly America – in promoting a more democratic system of world governance. Will the UN Security Council be modified with this in mind?

8.2.2 The direction of innovation

The techno-scientific boom is a rule of the game. What remains uncertain, however, is the direction that this spring tide of innovation is going to take. In the same way that nuclear energy can power whole cities while nuclear weapons can destroy them in seconds, we are increasingly faced with ethical choices in our use of technology. Some types of biotechnology can help clean up pollution, while other kinds increase the dependence of already marginalised farmers on multinational chemical companies. On the one hand more powerful personal computers, combined with faster Internet access, has enabled small business to carve out global niches in a way that would have been impossible twenty

167

years ago. On the other hand, software development in procurement programmes has allowed large companies to rationalise the number of their suppliers, which has resulted in many small companies being struck off the list.

Hence, although technology is neutral to some extent, the direction in which we develop and apply it is anything but neutral. Consider the current debate on the pros and cons of genetically modified food, or the cloning of human beings, for example. Guided by the principles of sustainability, some of these dilemmas become less ambiguous. Expand the use of carbon-based fuels by subsidisation, or invest in renewable energy? The former is environmentally unsustainable, so the answer is obvious. Install high tech manufacturing facilities in a country with high unemployment, or support labour-intensive methods? The former is socially unsustainable, so the solution is self-evident. Or at least it should be in the future. The uncertainty lies in the extent to which governments and financial markets and ordinary consumers are going to support this trend towards sustainable technology.

8.2.3 *Economic and trade policy developments*

Will we see economic reforms that put a cost on environmental degradation through eco-taxes? Or that help to lift people out of the poverty trap through basic income grants? Will speculators be given free reign to wreak havoc with international markets and national economies, or will they be reigned in through 'Tobin taxes'? Will 'parallel currencies' be supported and promoted as a way of empowering local communities? How will we balance the interests of pension funds, life insurance companies and other institutional shareholders who need gains in share prices to run their businesses effectively against the need to create incentives for companies to become more elephant-like in their approach to *all* stakeholders? Will the monetary system be adapted to give greater access to capital to entrepreneurs and communities, or will excessively high interest rates and the overhang of foreign debt continue to thwart economic development in Third World countries? The difficulties experienced by Argentina highlight how significant this key uncertainty is.

Likewise, the way in which the rules of international trade evolve will either support lion-like behaviour or be sensitive to elephants' needs. The World Trade Organisation smacks of an exclusive feline club – established by the already dominant players with only their own interests in mind. Will it pry open new markets no matter what the cost is to the vulnerable countries concerned? Or will it be counterbalanced by the fair trade movement which is more concerned with sharing the benefits of trade equitably and sustainably? On a different note, will sustainability-oriented certification and labelling schemes become part and parcel of the international trading system in order to allow trading partners to differentiate between lion and elephant companies?

8.2.4 *Political maturity*

If countries were children, we would not hesitate to tell some of them, in no uncertain terms, to stop their petty squabbles and temper tantrums, to cut out their selfish, brattish behaviour and to quit their senseless, destructive ranting. The disquieting flare-up of nationalistic, regional, cultural and religious rivalries is a key uncertainty that can destroy all the best intentions for a sustainable world. Whether it is Zimbabwe's troubles, the Middle Eastern conflict, Ireland's bloody sibling rivalry or the West versus Islam, the threat to social and environmental sustainability is very real.

To create a sustainable future, politicians and countries

will need to grow up. They have to be big enough to put their ideological differences aside, to allow wounds of the past to heal, and to realise that the only viable future is one in which everybody compromises to keep the peace and share the prosperity. This may sound like starry-eyed, wishful thinking, but that's exactly how the political miracle brokered between Mandela and De Klerk in South Africa sounded in the early 1990s. Then again, as any parent will attest, children are a notoriously unpredictable lot, and some never seem to grow up!

In the global kindergarten, the possibility of some regional conflict getting out of hand – for example India and Pakistan or Israel and Iraq ending up in a nuclear exchange – is considerable. We don't have the two 'teachers' that we used to have in charge of the 'classroom'. When a regional dispute arose during the old 'Cold War' days, America took one side and the Soviet Union the other and somehow they contained the situation. Even when we came close to nuclear war over the Cuban missile crisis, sense prevailed in the end. Nowadays, America does not want to commit its young men to conflicts which have nothing to do with America's interests, Russia has troubles of its own and the United Nations is simply too weak and too stretched to cope. Against this backdrop nuclear proliferation continues unchecked, which means that the boys in the classroom have some very dangerous toys.

8.2.5 *The rate of environmental decline*

The current decline of virtually every ecosystem on the planet is only in dispute by those who choose, usually for conveniently selfish reasons, to turn a blind eye to the overwhelming body of scientific evidence that is mounting up day by day. Facts and figures aside, it is common sense. Virtually every substance on earth is a potential poison – it is just a matter of concentration. In other words, there is a certain threshold beyond which almost all substances are toxic to life, including the human body. Since everything on earth disperses, but nothing disappears, our biggest problem is that persistent substances (like many chemicals and heavy metals) are steadily building up in our environment. It is only a matter of time before they become 'toxic'.

We are reminded of the African tale of the Earth Mother placing a fig tree into the care of a troop of monkeys. However, the monkeys not only ate the fruit, they stripped the bark and broke off the branches as well. In other words, they went beyond reasonable greed. When the Earth Mother returned, the fig tree had withered and died and the skeletons of the monkeys lay scattered on the ground.

What is uncertain is the rate of environmental decline, and exactly when we will start to feel the system biting back – when crop yields will plummet; or fishing stocks pass the point of no return; or wild swings in weather patterns become the norm; or chemicals in the environment start manifesting as health defects in humans. The Natural Step calls these feedback loops "hitting the walls of the funnel". Another uncertainty is whether it will be too late to take corrective action by the time the problem becomes obvious. For instance, even if the whole world stopped emitting greenhouse gases tomorrow, we would still feel the effects of the damage already done for centuries to come. Will we be like the many species which perished in the last ice age? By the time they noticed the temperature change, they could not adapt quickly enough.

8.2.6 *Social unrest*

The past hundred years of industrial development have been building up to a situation of intolerable social inequity. The widening gap between the 'haves' and 'have-nots', now exacerbated by the digital divide, is a breeding ground for social discontent. We should be heeding the lessons of history. After all, how many popular revolts have been directed against unjust rule and too great a concentration of wealth and power? And yet, this is exactly the kind of situation we find in our world today: between the First and Third Worlds, between billionaire tycoons and slave-wage workers, between the Wabenzi (Mercedes-driving politicians) and their starving, unemployed constituents.

Are the anti-globalisation protests of Seattle and the terror attacks of September 11 merely a hint of what is to come? How much longer will the billions of poor people in Third World countries put their faith in the hollow promises of the 'trickle down' economics of globalisation? Can the materialistic goals of American free-market capitalism ever be reconciled with the cultural traditions of the Islamic Middle East? We are at a critical stage in the world's history, somewhere just below boiling point, when a few degrees one way or the other could make all the difference – the difference between social unrest boiling over or simmering down.

However, there is something that moves social unrest straight up the uncertainty charts to a prime position: the change in the mathematics of destruction. It is now quite possible for some shadowy cult of extremely evil people to gain access to weapons of mass destruction – nuclear, biological or chemical. $E = mc^2$ is a genie which will never be put back in the bottle. Extremist cults and terrorist organisations will exploit social unrest as a launch pad for their evil deeds. Thus, a requirement for a peaceful world is a level of social stability which allows nations to cooperate in establishing an effective global intelligence network against such criminals.

8.2.7 *Lifestyle choices*

The simple illusion of lion-friendly capitalism that has kept most of the world under a spell for the past fifty years is that 'we can have our cake and eat it'. Even sustainable development is twisted by politicians to mean that more economic growth will solve our social and environmental problems. However, when US President George W. Bush pulls out of the Kyoto Protocol agreement on climate change because it will hurt the American economy, we are left in no doubt as to the illusion that we are asked to accept. A switch to an elephant economy *will* require short-term sacrifices and investments that will only pay off down the line.

The key uncertainty is whether individuals and companies and countries will follow a path leading to sustainable lifestyles, or whether we will shun the short-term sacrifices necessary for long-term environmental integrity and social wellbeing. How many of us will pay extra cash to have a catalytic converter fitted onto our car's exhaust? How many of us can afford it? Will our companies combat HIV / AIDS by making the required investment in educational programmes leading to behavioural change and the infrastructure required to deliver antiretroviral drugs to employees and the community? Will our politicians eliminate perverse subsidies relating to unsustainable lifestyles and direct these towards social banking and renewable energy? There are a multitude of lifestyle choices that will shape our future.

8.3 *Scenarios*

Given the rules of the game and the key uncertainties just described, we have chosen two contrasting scenarios to illustrate how the future landscape of business and the world could turn out. As mentioned already, the actual outcome will partly depend on the options we choose over the coming decade. The two scenarios are: (1) *Oases in the Desert*;

and (2) *Plains of the Serengeti*. Remember, scenarios are stories of what *can* happen in the future – they are *not* forecasts of what is going to happen. Their purpose is to educate rather than prescribe.

8.3.1 *Oases in the Desert*

Oases in the Desert is where we end up if the lions continue on their path of ascendancy towards global domination. The scenario's oasis image points to pockets of plenty existing in the midst of a desert of deprivation. It is almost as if the excesses of water and lush greenery in the oasis have been sucked out of the rest of the landscape and accumulated at just a few spots. Some golf courses give one that impression! Generally, the scenario is the net result of the present lions' tendency to accumulate power and concentrate wealth in fewer and fewer hands (or should that be paws?). Additional consequences are that the majority of the world's population is pushed into a marginal existence and the natural environment is systematically degraded.

Only the cats get fatter. Like black holes in astronomy, wealth becomes so condensed that it creates its own 'singularity of greed'. All the money that flows into the lions' den never escapes. Not surprisingly, the nationality of the current members of the den is mainly American. The richest of them all – Walton not Gates – is worth over one hundred billion dollars or more than a trillion rand. And guess what? Elephants are few and far between in this terrain. The US gives away far less of its GDP on good causes than other nations; and only a miniscule proportion finds its way overseas. As we mentioned earlier, generosity is regarded by lions as a sign of weakness.

Those that are familiar with Frank Herbert's bestselling science fiction series, *Dune*, will have no difficulty imagining the scene. The story is set on the desert planet of Arakas,

174

the sole source of spice, which is a mineral on which the galactic population is dependent. The mercenary tycoons that control the spice control the universe, and they're not about to share their accrued benefits of power, wealth and water with anybody else.

At first, the lion kings – individuals, businesses and politicians that have exploited the current global situation relentlessly for their own selfish gain – may revel in their opulence without concern. They will think that they are simply collecting their just reward for being superior players of the modern game of material gain. Most likely, their mesmerised fans will worship them as heroes. They will form exclusive clubs where only royalty is welcome, so that they can show off their treasures to one another, strategise about how they can shape the destiny of the world and re-assure one another that they deserve everything they've got. Occasionally, they will fall out with one another and have trade wars, but they never allow these differences to jeopardise their overall control.

Their self-indulgent lives will lack only one thing – peace of mind. Because, as everyone knows, water is a priceless commodity in the desert. And if you own and control the water supply, all those billions that are dying of thirst in the desert will do desperate things to gain access to the fountain, or just to vent their stored-up hatred – they may even commit murder! Therefore, security will become a primary and constant concern for lions. High walls, alarm systems, bodyguards, hidden vaults, police investigators, secret escape tunnels, private armies, you name it: they will install and employ them. But they will never feel completely safe. Lingering in the background will always be the fear of the next crazed suicide bomber or undetected anthrax delivery.

Of course, the lion kings will own what is left of the living environment – all the most pristine ecological reserves will be their exclusive playground. Their homes, their offices and their vehicles will be fitted with all the latest technological wizardry to insulate them from the pervasive pollution and saturation of toxins that incessantly plague the masses. And yet there will still be some things that they just can't buy or own or control. The unpredictable weather patterns will continue to be an expensive source of irritation, as will the seemingly random collapse of shares in their portfolio when the company or the industry in which they are invested is implicated in the latest health scare, fatal accident or environmental disaster.

The era of the lion kings will not last forever and it will probably end with a bang or a squelch. As the vast majority of the world's population sees the gap ever widening between their own poverty-ridden and environmentally-degraded existence and the insular wealth of rich executives, large multinationals and First World countries, a global mass protest movement gathers momentum and becomes increasingly volatile and violent, eventually making the kingdom of the lion king ungovernable. This popular discontent is exacerbated as ecosystems continue to topple like dominoes, and the most vulnerable populations begin to suffer the ravages of pollution-induced disease. Terror strikes against lion countries as well as lion companies become more common, fuelled by cultural and religious tensions. Ultimately, such developments lead to a chain reaction that descends into full-scale nuclear and biochemical warfare. A selection of oases meet their doomsdays ahead of schedule. You may recall our reference to butterfly wings causing the perfect storm if conditions are right – a tiny little thing triggering off a huge response. Maybe the few hundred vote difference in Florida in the last US presidential election will be responsible for the Third World War. Who knows?

Plains of the Serengeti is where we head for if the lions realise that their game of domination has a no-win conclusion and voluntarily or begrudgingly begin shapeshifting into elephants. The scenario conjures up breathtaking images of the fertile plains of East Africa and the Great Rift Valley teeming with wildlife, all living in a state of dynamic harmony with each other and the natural environment. A rich heritage of biological diversity exists, with even the predators finding their rightful place within the larger community of animals. Hence, although competition still takes place in the society, it is tempered by the more pervasive cooperative tendency in Nature which ensures that a healthy balance is maintained. The smaller, more entrepreneurial animals flourish in this setting.

The trail leading to the *Serengeti* requires that at various levels of society, from the individual through to the community, from business through to the economy, from politics through to global governance, a consensus emerges regarding new rules of the game that are in everyone's collective interest, including criteria for ecological sustainability and minimum equity requirements for social sustainability. As a consequence of these new governance principles, the sixth mass species extinction and the poisoning of the environment are halted and reversed, and the formerly marginalised and disempowered sections of the world's population are given a fair stake in global society and the economy.

Much of the success of the transition to a sustainable world has to do with the restructuring of the economy. The incentive mechanisms are redesigned in such a way that excessive accumulation of wealth and concentration of power are strongly discouraged, negative environmental impacts are prohibitively expensive and meeting social needs is a primary condition for operating at any level in the economy. Money still exists, but shapeshifts into a multitiered commodity with community currencies being created as and when required as a means of facilitating local exchange of goods. Modifications to the interest and discount rate mechanisms are devised, and speculation is heavily taxed. The main difference from the lion trail is that the economy is made to serve people and the environment and not the other way round.

Business still plays a critical role in the world, meeting people's needs with its products and services; but the power and influence that it previously had over global affairs is now subject to numerous social, environmental and ethical checks and balances. While an important purpose of companies remains the making of profit and the provision of a return to shareholders, their overall objective is widened to that of making a permanent contribution in the communities in which they operate. Work itself is seen as a means to an end, a 'space' in which people can develop their potential, express their talents and make a positive contribution to society. Survival is no longer dependent on having a formal job. Most places of work and living are digitally connected, with an emphasis on decentralising as much authority as possible to employees and providing them with congenial surroundings.

Among the fundamental principles that are embedded in society in this scenario are creative diversity, freedom with accountability and the philosophy of holism. At the same time, the technological revolution continues apace and more and more is directed towards meeting human needs and ensuring ecological sustainability. Moreover, it is matched by a corresponding revolution in the outlook of humans towards their planet. The new wave of discovery will be focused on understanding the physiology and psychology of healthy living systems (including all levels of human interaction) and developing the personal and social skills to build these systems effectively. However, given the fact that the actual Serengeti is home to both elephants *and* lions, it would be wrong to typecast a scenario named after it as an elephant heaven devoid of all lions. You will still have highly competitive companies operating in the lion mode – but the rules of the park won't favour them anymore.

Put another way, the *Serengeti* scenario contains digital satellite television with the lions watching sport, CNN and Bloomberg, while the elephants prefer National Geographic and Discovery. But the younger generation will do more channel-hopping and hopefully obtain a more balanced view of the world than their parents.

8.4 *Options*

Having depicted the possible paths that the future can take in two mainline scenarios, we must now consider the options within the control of the principal actors, which will increase or reduce the probabilities of either scenario materialising. While we will concentrate on the options facing companies, multilevel shapeshifting makes it essential to bring countries and individuals into the picture. At the business level, we have nominated the three options:

(1) *Catwalk*; (2) *Leophancy*; and (3) *The Charge of the Heavy Brigade*.

8.4.1 *Catwalk*

The first option for companies is to continue down the *Catwalk*. In other words, it's business as usual with the lions on the prowl. Sustained pressure from shareholders and the sanctity of the profit motive will continue the drive towards greater efficiencies, the expansion into new markets and the accumulation of capital. Repeated mergers and acquisitions will be necessary to secure survival, until eventually global industries are dominated by just a handful of multinational corporations. In order to facilitate the unrestricted operation of global companies and their access to potential markets, initiatives like the World Trade Organisation and the Multilateral Agreement on Investments will be strongly supported. Any criticism of these global 'rules of trade' will be called foulplay and an attempt to resist the levelling of the playing fields (which are anything but level).

The concept of stakeholders will be acknowledged, but a strict hierarchy of priority will be applied. Directors, shareholders and financial institutions will continue to take precedence over any other group. Employees and customers get the attention they need to ensure the successful sale of the companies' products and services. Other groups, like government, communities, media and environmental or social activists will be treated as necessary evils, to be negotiated with or influenced as and when required. A minimum level of charitable work and social and environmental contributions will be maintained to project the public image of a responsible corporate citizen. However, should any business decision require a trade-off between economic returns and social impacts or environmental degradation, the colour of money will always win the day.

Corporate executives will rise to the status of kings in a changing landscape of growing disparity. For most business directors and line managers, their actions will remain within the boundaries of the law as they steadily accumulate great fortunes of wealth. Given the rules of the free-market game, they will simply be regarded as extremely talented players who are collecting their hard-earned and well-deserved prize of gold. The plight of the world's poor and the steady decline in global environmental conditions will be seen as problems for government or the United

Nations to take care of (after all, that's what taxes are for!). Despite the waves of layoffs as industries consolidate, technologies improve and efficiencies go up, *Catwalk* managers will continue to argue that their contribution steadily trickles down to benefit everyone. Whatever happens, they consider this argument unassailable.

To illustrate the *Catwalk* option further, corporate responses to the climate change debate have been truly revealing. The biggest animals in the pride – including BP Amoco, Chevron, Daimler Chrysler, Exxon Mobil, Ford Motor Company, General Motors, Royal Dutch Shell and Texaco – initially gathered together under the umbrella of the Global Climate Coalition. The express objective of this grouping was to dispute and discredit the scientific basis of climate change and the global agreement being formulated to regulate greenhouse gas emissions (the Kyoto Protocol). It comes as no surprise that these companies are massive emitters of greenhouse gases, and that any regulation of this source of pollution would be extremely costly for them to implement. Interestingly, some of these lions have since shown signs of trimming their whiskers, which is a fitting introduction to the next option.

8.4.2 *Leophancy*

Like sycophants, leophants want to be all things to all people – sucking up to the shareholders when it suits them and rolling over for the 'greenies' when circumstances demand. They have recognised that some of their lion traits are going to get them into trouble sooner or later and that elephants are beginning to gain favour in the world. As a result, they are just starting to test the water – introducing an environmental policy here, adopting a corporate governance code there, adding a few nonfinancial performance measures, setting up community forums. They are not yet bold enough

181

to whip off their lion suits and dive right into the refreshing pool of sustainability. After all, there may be sharp objects lurking beneath the surface; besides, other lions might laugh if they discover that their roar is bigger than their ... well, you know!

Leophants feel a little schizophrenic, as a result of being caught between two worlds. Their sensitive radar systems are picking up large grey blobs in the distance, but the growl of lions much closer by resonates in their ears. On the one hand, they hear the muffled cries of angry special interest groups; on the other the ticking of the share price is difficult to ignore. They can feel their ears starting to flap, their noses beginning to droop and their incisors about to protrude from their mouths, but they are a little embarrassed or scared to come out of the closet. Although they are aware of a few lone elephants in the desert, they have seen prides of lion take down some of these brave pioneers. Better just to hide out in the shadows, hedge the bets and play it safe.

Becoming a leophant is not necessarily the easiest option. Like an adolescent tripping into puberty, leophant companies risk looking awkward and ungainly. Their management and staff feel that every decision is now riddled with paradox and uncertainty. Apart from this, if the economy, political scene and the financial markets are not shapeshifting at the same rate, there is always the danger of being heavily criticised by the Greek chorus of fund managers in the background. Hence, leophants often begin with small elephant-friendly actions, but cover them up by still growling loudly like one of the old macho pride. They feel an incessant compulsion to justify their every move towards sustainability by saying that there is a business case for it, or that their actions are nothing more than good risk management.

Picking up on our climate change example, it has been

fascinating to watch how some of the founding members of the Global Climate Coalition – such as BP Amoco, Ford, Shell and Texaco – have since defected. Following this change of heart, first BP and then Shell committed themselves publicly to reducing greenhouse gases, pioneered internal emissions trading systems and upped their investments in renewable energy. Likewise, under its new chairman Bill Ford, the family's motor manufacturing giant has suddenly become very vocal about its preparations for leadership in a post-fossil-fuel-based economy. *Leophancy* is catching on! Much of the inspiration for it comes from those who are less cautious in their approach to sustainability issues, and that brings us to our final option.

8.4.3 *The Charge of the Heavy Brigade*

Elephant jokes were all the rage in the 1960s. One went as follows: what do you do if a herd of elephant is thundering towards you? Answer: make a trunk call and reverse the charge! However, so as not to undermine our support for elephants we have to tell a lion joke as well. Van der Merwe was walking through the Kruger National Park with his friend Koos. Koos asks: "Why are you wearing the latest Nike running shoes with air-cushioning and ankle support?" Van replies: "Because I don't want to get eaten by a lion." Koos laughs and says: "But you won't be able to outrun a lion." Van looks at Koos who tips the scales at 100 kilograms and grins: "No Koos, all I have to do is outrun you!"

More seriously, the final option for companies is to blaze a trail for the sustainable future by wholeheartedly and unashamedly joining *The Charge of the Heavy Brigade*. Strength lies in numbers, and the greater the number of companies that make the switch from lions to elephants, the less they will be dismissed as mavericks. One lonely elephant trumpeting in the bush is not enough! Moreover, the public will find it refreshing to have a growing constituency of corporate leaders driven by a sense of values, purpose and destiny. Their zealous mission will be to show that it is not only possible, but essential, to transform businesses into an elephant-friendly force in society – an agent of change for good. It is not uncommon for CEOs pursuing the elephant option to have had some kind of 'revelation' about how unsustainable the traditional business model really is. They suddenly 'get it'; and they realise that life is not so much about making money as making a difference. Then instead of shouting about their conversion from the rooftops, they quietly go ahead and change their lifestyle accordingly.

One of the first actions of elephant pioneers is to shut up and start listening. They quickly establish various mechanisms for comprehensively surveying and understanding the complex needs of their numerous stakeholders. They also put in place a series of indicators to track their corporate performance in terms of these needs. However, as they begin to tune their senses to the incoming infrasonic messages, they realise that good communication is often not about the 'letter' but the 'spirit' of what is being said in return. They also realise that dealing effectively with stakeholders only works if power is balanced and shared. It cannot work if shareholders' selfish demands always take precedence over community or environmental concerns. Nor should customers' willingness to consume a harmful product or service necessarily imply that it should be produced and sold. Elephants will find that they are constantly required to revise their preconceived notions about the way that businesses *should* be run, and the valuable role that different stakeholder groups *can* play.

At the moment, the herd of fellow elephant-oriented companies is still relatively small. They therefore find themselves often mingling with NGOs and activists. This network of passionate comrades are their source of inspiration and 'insider' information. They give the company clues as to what issues are ticking time bombs and what products are hot prospects for a sustainable future. They act like a weather barometer, signalling how the mood of the sustainability debate is subtly shifting and what direction to head in to find sunshine and avoid the thunderstorms. Sometimes, these activist groups sit on corporate advisory boards or performance review panels. Elephant companies soon discover that their advice, more often than not, has its roots in a deep caring for people and the planet.

Returning to our climate change example, companies on the elephant trail actively support the phasing out of greenhouse gases and a shift to a hydrogen and solar economy. Not overnight, but over time. A case in point is OK Petroleum, Sweden's largest refiner and retailer of gasoline, who joined with twenty-four other companies to lobby the government to *increase* carbon taxes. This was partially due to the fact that OK had already shapeshifted far enough to design a low-carbon gasoline. But it was also because OK no longer sees itself as being in the petroleum business – it is a clean energy company of the future. Inevitably, the real elephant companies find themselves shifting their investments out of socially sensitive, environmentally-damaging businesses into more sustainable sectors and technologies.

8.5 Decisions

We don't know which option you will choose or what decisions you will make as a result of reading this book. But we can certainly offer you some tips. If you're a CEO, the best thing you can probably do is go through the line of reasoning that we've followed in this chapter at your company's next strategic planning session. This time, however, you get some unusual stakeholders to join you who might offer different perspectives on the future rules of the environmental and social game. Not just the generic ones that apply to business in general, but the specific ones that apply to your industry. You don't stifle the debate or try to steer it in the direction of your own vision. You just let it run where it will.

An alternative approach is to split your top management team into two or three small groups and ask each group to come up with *their* rules. It's amazing how different the results can be, leaving the CEO scratching his or her head that these people are in the same team and supposedly playing the same game. Add in one or two outsiders to each group and the results can be even more surprising when they are compared in the plenary session. The prime purpose, of course, of putting the executive team through this hoop is to get across to its leo-leaning members that there *are* rules beyond their control. They will get shocked by an electric fence if they go too far. Even the supreme CEO, Jack Welch, singed his whiskers late in life when General Electric's bid to acquire Honeywell was blocked by the European Commission. There are always limits; and business can be *unusual* at the best and worst of times.

As far as the key uncertainties are concerned, it is vital to emphasise that this is a 'blue sky' discussion and no uncertainty can be too wild to consider. Back in 1986, HIV / AIDS was classified by a South African scenario team as a 'wild card' that might affect the country's future. It quickly became a primary rule of the game. In other words, a faint dot on the radar screen may emerge as the biggest threat.

Scenarios function as a bridging mechanism between the external world you don't control and the internal one that you do. Their purpose is to synthesise all the information contained in the rules of the game and the key uncertainties into two or three simple stories that the mind can grasp when making a decision. Scenarios are the narrow part of the hourglass. Using this principle, one of the two authors presented South Africans with a stark but easily understandable choice back in the mid-1980s: *The High Road* of negotiation leading to a political settlement or *The Low Road* of confrontation leading to a civil war and a wasteland. As CEO, you want to stimulate to your colleagues by depicting a set of clear-cut scenarios that differentiate between lion and elephant behaviour and the consequences for the company.

The discussion of options available to a company is where the bottom of the hourglass widens out again. It should be as 'blue sky' as the conversation about uncertainties. If anybody says that such-and-such an option is far too wild, you can perfectly reasonably retort that it's just an option with no commitment. Remember that options are not a wish list. Each one is a decision you can take and implement right now if you decide to select that option. Again, outsiders are a valuable resource in broadening the terms of the debate.

Lastly, you make decisions which we hope after all the arguments we have presented in this book will point you down the elephant trail. And just as you start down a hiking trail with that first step, don't be too ambitious at the beginning. The initial step taken by a company should be to establish a process, which means that each subsequent step is chosen with the new philosophy in mind: that of being a 'sustainable business'. Like elephants in the mist, you will never know in advance where the trail ultimately leads. Sometimes you will take wrong steps and you will have to reverse direction to get back on the path again. On other occasions, a single step will take you around a corner where a breathtaking view awaits you. And when you look back over your shoulder, you will wonder how you managed to come so far. But if you take no steps at all, the future has a nasty habit of catching up with you.

8.6 *Multilevel shapeshifting revisited*

So, we are now at the conclusion of the book. As the young would say, we've given it horns – or perhaps that should be tusks! – in order to get a simple message across: our choices today will to a large extent shape our future landscape, whether it be *Oases in the Desert* or *Plains of the Serengeti*. Nevertheless, it bears repeating that our own choices as company executives and individuals are undeniably influenced by the direction of the choices being made at a political level. If the entire industrialised world takes its cue from the current signals coming out of America, it will be very difficult for anything but the lion-oriented scenario to emerge. On the other hand, should a critical mass of powerful countries or regions take sustainability more seriously, the elephant-oriented future starts to look more likely. But it cannot be overemphasised enough that the United States as the biggest animal in the park has to join the herd eventually. The worst outcome would be for America to turn from being a lion into a rogue elephant, thereby continuing to put its own self-interest above everybody else's, but with a little more guile. We live in *one world* and the United States will never be a true winner if it is surrounded by resentful losers. Alas, there are plenty of the latter at the moment.

Our climate change example may be useful just once more here. With George W. Bush on its back, the American Jumbo withdrew for purely selfish reasons from the Kyoto Protocol – a multilateral agreement that had taken the world ten years to negotiate and which America had already signed (but not ratified). We may look back on this showdown as a crucial turning point in history. If any one of the world's powerful nations had sided with the United

States, the Protocol would have collapsed and set us back fifty years on the path to sustainability. But the entire world took a stand *against* America and *for* the Kyoto Protocol and a more elephant-friendly future. As the title of our book suggests, we do not expect humankind to dispense entirely with its selfish side. We will always want some measure of success in material and spiritual terms for ourselves and our families. But when an individual, a family, a clan or a nation pursues its self-interest to the point of unreasonable greed, the whole system risks collapse as acquisition becomes plunder. And the only difference between a plundering dictator and a plundering director is technique.

Don't misunderstand us. America is *not* what is wrong with the world, but it can surely do better as the world's leading nation. To start with, it can set a better example in not being so lion-like and then having everyone else wanting to emulate it (like the City of London). Success: yes – greed: no. Then it can do a lot more to help to create a win-win environment and make the world a more inclusive place. We have all heard of the American dream: the idea that anybody can become a 'somebody' in the land of freedom and opportunity. That dream will end in tatters if it doesn't become more universally applicable – to anybody anywhere in the world.

But governments can't do everything. Ordinary people also hold the fragile destiny of our globe in their hands. Every time a person fixes a leaking tap, plants a tree, buys organic produce or switches off the lights when going out for the evening, he or she is helping the human race to shapeshift towards ecological integrity. And each time someone campaigns against human rights abuses, buys fair trade goods, or joins the neighbourhood watch, he or she is taking us just that little bit closer to social harmony. Individuals *do* make a difference, little things *do* count.

We believe we are passing on a timeless message, wrapped in an enduring symbol. After all, Rome's renowned natural historian Pliny wrote more than two thousand years ago: "Elephants are receptive to love and renown and possess the virtues of honesty, consideration and justice to a higher degree than the majority of men."

Today, we find 20th Century Fox conveying essentially the same message in their recent blockbuster animated movie *The Ice Age*. Only, the film uses slightly different words. The story tells of the journey of Manfred the woolly mammoth and his furry companions – Sid the sloth, Scrat the sabre-toothed squirrel and Diego the sabre-toothed tiger – during the great pre-freeze migration. While Diego is secretly leading Manfred into an ambush where his fellow predators lie hungrily in wait, Manfred ends up saving Diego's life. Dumbfounded, Diego asks why he would do such an unselfish thing. "That's what you do in a herd", replies the surprised Manfred. Then, right at the end of the movie, Diego has the opportunity to return the favour by saving Manfred's life. Implying that he has managed to shapeshift beyond his selfish predatory instincts and adopt the more caring nature of an elephant, he shrugs off Manfred's gratitude by repeating back to him his own words of wisdom: "That's what you do in a herd!"

In a similar vein, we hope we have persuaded some of you to do the honourable thing and trade in your fangs for tusks.